's Day

1969

with love from Shird

BYRON

and his world

BYRON

and his world

BY DEREK PARKER

A STUDIO BOOK

THE VIKING PRESS · NEW YORK

TO JULIA

'What I think of myself is, that I am so changable, being everything by turns and nothing long, – I am such a strange *mélange* of good and evil, that it would be difficult to describe me.'

Byron quoted by Lady Blessington, *The Idler in Italy* (1839)

Published in 1969 by The Viking Press, Inc., 625 Madison Avenue, New York, N.Y. 10022

Library of Congress Catalog Card Number: 69–10355

Printed in Great Britain by Jarrold and Sons Ltd, Norwich, England

Newstead Abbey, *c.* 1720 · *It was a vast and venerable pile;*
So old, it seemed only not to fall,
Yet strength was pillar'd in each massy aisle....

IF BYRON was handsome, witty, radical, a brilliant conversationalist, and at his best also a brilliant poet, it is also true that he was cruel, petty, amoral, quick-tempered and proud. Some of these latter traits may well have been hereditary, although the family's eccentricities did not really develop until relatively late in its history.

The first recorded ancestor of Byron's was Radulfus de Burun, who appears in Domesday Book, and Newstead Abbey was associated with the family after the dissolution of the monasteries, when Henry VIII sold 'all the house and site, ground and soil, of the late Monastery or Priory of Newstede within the Forest of Sherewood in our said County of Nottingham' to Sir John Byron, for a nominal £810. A later Sir John, a general of Charles I, was created Baron Byron of Rochdale in 1643, and the family lost most of its property during the ensuing Civil War.

It was the fifth Lord Byron, born in 1722, who became known as 'the Wicked
Lord', and whose various extravagances (including the mounting of naval
battles in the moat at Newstead, and the notorious killing of a neighbour, William
Chaworth, in a duel) were remembered even by Byron's contemporaries. The
Wicked Lord's son, Byron's grandfather, eloped with his first cousin, and joined
the Navy, becoming an Admiral (nicknamed 'Foulweather Jack' by his crews).
There were certain scandals attached to his name; but these were far outreached
by the scandals attached to the name of his son (and Byron's father) John, who
was born at Plymouth in 1756.

A profligate and a gambler, John Byron had scarcely been bought a commission
in the Guards, when he seduced the beautiful and rich wife of Lord Carmarthen.
She obtained a divorce, and he married her, and lived for the six years of their
marriage in France, where they had three children – the only survivor of whom
was Augusta, who was born in 1783.

Finding that his wife's income ceased at her death, Captain Byron set off for
England, obviously in search of another heiress. Wisely, he went to Bath, where
the most fashionable families stayed in the season. This was the great age of the
spa, and at Bath (or Harrogate, or Tunbridge Wells) were to be found not only
aristocrats, but rich families of the upper middle class who, if they were *very* rich,
were greeted on their arrival by a peal of bells.

◀ Bath, The Circus, at the end
of the eighteenth century

Mrs Byron. 'A tender and
peremptory parent who
indulged me sometimes with
holidays and now and then
with a box on the ear.'

*Father and
Mother*

It is not recorded whether the bells welcomed to Bath a twenty-year-old Scottish
girl, Catherine Gordon – an orphan with a fortune of £20,000. Elegant and
dashing, Captain Byron had no difficulty in capturing her; and they were married
on 13 May 1785.

Byron's mother was as unattractive as his father was charming: vulgar, plump
and plain, an illiterate gossip, she had a passionate temper and a coarse tongue –
her family, of Gight, thirty miles north of Aberdeen, had a record of violence and
lawlessness dating from the sixteenth century, and almost unparalleled even in
the Scotland of their time. One of her few virtues was her love for her husband;
but it was a virtue that literally ruined her, for by 1786 Captain Byron had spent
the £3,000 in cash that his wife had at hand, and had mortgaged her estate for
£8,000. A year later Gight was sold to pay his debts; but even so bailiffs followed
the couple around England, and they were forced to take refuge in Paris in 1787.
The beginnings of unrest were already being felt there, and when Catherine
Byron became pregnant, she decided to travel to London to have her child.

7

Byron's birthplace,
16 Holles Street

(*below*) A view of
St Marylebone Church

8

Castle Street, Aberdeen

And so it was that Byron was born in London, on 22 January 1788, in a *Byron's birth* furnished back room at 16 Holles Street – a lane which ran between Oxford Street and Cavendish Square, all traces of which vanished in the blitz of 1940 (although the street-name is preserved). By this time, his father too was in England; but he had to remain in hiding from his creditors, and was not at Marylebone Parish Church on 29 February, when his son was christened George Gordon Byron.

After almost a year in hiding in London, Mrs Byron took her child and travelled north to Aberdeen, to the country she knew. There she prepared to live on £150 a year – the income from the remains of the capital realized by the sale of Gight. Captain Byron followed her, and they settled in cramped rooms in Queen Street. John and Catherine irritated each other, and the baby irritated them both; John left his wife – to live at the other end of Queen Street, from which he paid her visits to beg for money. In September 1790, just after her regular allowance had arrived, he disappeared to France, taking with him every penny

9

Byron aged seven
Few are my years, and yet I feel
The world was ne'er design'd for me.

(*opposite*) Aberdeen Grammar School
'might consist of one hundred and
fifty of all aged under age.
It was divided into five classes,
taught by four masters.'

he could find. While his wife lived virtually penniless in Aberdeen, he spent freely in Valenciennes, managing (it seems) to ignore the French Revolution which raged and spluttered around him. Eventually, even his talent for fraud and procrastination ran out; and he died, quite suddenly, on 2 August 1791. His enormous charm had never failed to captivate his wife, who wrote to his sister: 'notwithstanding all his foibles . . . I ever sincerely loved him.'

So, during his earlier years, Byron experienced only poverty, the ill-temper of his mother, and the absence of a father – although he could just recollect the noise and violence of his parents' arguments, and 'had very early a horror of matrimony, from the sight of domestic broils.'

One should not forget that, despite her failings, Catherine Byron loved her son, in her own fashion – and was particularly concerned about his one physical ailment: he had been born with a deformed left foot. Whether he had a club foot, or whether the fault was merely in a shortened tendon, has been a matter for conjecture ever since his death; and it is doubtful whether the question will ever be resolved. But whatever the distortion was, Catherine Byron set herself resolutely to remedy it. She consulted doctors as soon as the child could walk, and she bought special boots in an attempt to correct the fault. Undoubtedly, the attention she focused on his foot made Byron himself extremely self-conscious about it. When, as he was out walking with his nurse, they met another nurse who remarked: 'What a pretty boy Byron is! What a pity he has such a leg!' – the four-year-old struck out at her with a toy whip, shouting: 'Dinna speak of it!' His sensitivity on the subject lasted all his life.

10

When he was five, the child was sent to his first school – a small mixed school very near his home in Broad Street. It seems to have been almost a slum school, but there were at least one or two sympathetic teachers, and soon Byron began to read; he was not much addicted to adventure stories, or the usual boys' books of the time, preferring (or at least so he said in later years) the *Arabian Nights*, *Don Quixote*, Smollett's *Roderick Random* and the Bible. It is often difficult to decide whether Byron is being precisely truthful when he speaks of himself; but whether or not he read Cervantes at the age of five, there is no doubt that he became very familiar with the Bible – and especially the Old Testament – at a very early age. Thirty years later he was able to confuse an ecclesiastical bore by the readiness with which he could quote from the Scriptures. And indeed it was when he was five or six that his lifelong preoccupation with the problem of predestination began fascinating him in the story of Cain and Abel. A Calvinist nurse underlined the gloom which swamped his first contacts with religion, and from these years onward he felt – certainly in his pessimistic moments – that he was predestined to some unpleasant end; that (as he wrote in *Childe Harold*)

> *life abhorring Gloom*
> *Wrote on his faded brow curst Cain's unresting doom.*

But in many respects his life was that of a normal, cheerful schoolboy. He left the infant school, and went to Aberdeen Grammar School, where he was said to be not over-addicted to study. He joined in the school games; swam in the estuary of the Dee; and when he was eight fell platonically but violently in love with a young distant cousin, Mary Duff.

Newstead Abbey, 1834   *Newstead! fast-falling, once-resplendent dome!*
Religion's shrine! repentant Henry's pride!
Of warriors, monks, and dames the cloister'd tomb,
Whose pensive shades around thy ruins glide,

Baron Byron   Then came the first important development of his external life. In 1893, Mrs
Byron had learned that the young grandson of the Wicked Lord had been killed
in Corsica, and that Byron was now the heir presumptive to the title. On 21 May
1898, the old Lord Byron died – and the ten-year-old boy became the sixth
Baron Byron of Rochdale, so embarrassed when his new title was spoken at
school roll-call that he burst into tears, and had to be sent home. The respectful
attitude of his master, however, 'gave him at once high notions of his new dignity'.

Hail to thy pile! more honour'd in thy fall
Than modern mansions in their pillar'd state;
Proudly majestic frowns thy vaulted hall,
Scowling defiance on the blasts of fate.

Mrs Byron intended to lose no time in claiming her, and her son's, rights. By August, she had sold her furniture, and left Scotland for Newstead. The reception that awaited the Byrons at the Abbey was not what she had expected. The old Lord had died in debt; the Abbey was almost in ruins, and almost empty – for most of the furniture had been seized by creditors. The outhouses were roofless, and cattle were stabled in the entrance hall. But, indefatigable, Mrs Byron moved in; and her attorney, John Hanson, started to clear up the financial mess.

View of a lane in Dulwich

Harrow Church and School from the cricket grounds
Again I revisit the hills where we sported,
The streams where we swam, and the fields where we fought. . . .

Young as he was, Byron very much enjoyed his ennobled position, once he had got used to it. Hanson brought him to London, and placed him at school at Dulwich. There, he paid little attention to work, and was quite unprepared for Harrow, where Hanson took him in April 1801. To be just, he had had little opportunity to concentrate on school work – his mother constantly interfered with it, and was always taking him to new doctors who had devised new and ever more painful treatments for his foot. And he had fallen again in love, with another cousin, Margaret Parker (who, he said later, inspired his 'first dash into poetry').

Byron seems to have lived a fairly normal life at Harrow: which means a tough and violent life. A school-fellow, Edward Noel Long, wrote home: 'There is another boy, Ld. Byrom, a lame fellow just come he seems a good sort of fellow.' Most of his school friends agreed; he was 'a good sort of fellow', prepared to fight a great deal, as one was expected to. He used regularly to beat one of his friends in order to persuade him to fight others 'when necessary as a point of honour and stature', and himself is said to have won six out of seven successive battles. No doubt his activities in this direction nurtured the taste for fighting which resulted in many friendships, later, with the pugilists of the times (he covered a screen with newspaper cuttings and engravings of them and their matches).

Harrow

Harrow school-room. 'I am very comfortable here as far as relates to my comrades, but I have got into two or three scrapes with Drury and the other masters, which are not very convenient. . . . But thank God they may call me a Blackguard, but they can never make me one.'

The churchyard at Harrow. 'There is a spot in the Churchyard, near the footpath, on the brow of the hill looking towards Windsor, and a tomb under a large tree (bearing the name Peachie, or Peachey), where I used to sit for hours and hours when a boy: this was my favourite spot.'

As to lessons – his quick wit carried him through them without too much trouble, and gradually he began to settle down, to become a little more thoughtful, and even – perhaps seated on his favourite tomb in Harrow churchyard – to write poetry.

His feelings for little Mary Duff and for Margaret Parker had been genuine and strong (abnormally strong for a boy of his age); but his first serious romance came when he was fifteen. He was staying at Newstead, and rode over to visit some neighbours at Annesley Hall, where he met the daughter of the house, Mary Chaworth (by coincidence, the descendant of the Wicked Lord's victim). She was eighteen; she was beautiful; she was engaged – and Byron fell instantly in love with her. He refused to return to Harrow, and rode over daily to Annesley.

16

Mary Chaworth
– Upon a tone,
A touch of hers, his blood would ebb and flow,
And his cheek change tempestuously. . . .

Augusta Leigh
Oh! blest be thy unbroken light!
That watch'd me as a seraph's eye,
And stood between me and the night. . . .

His love was desperate, serious, and he never forgot it. Yet it was not without bitterness: Mary felt little for him, and he overheard her, one day, say to her maid: 'Do you think I could care anything for that lame boy?'

Although he returned to Harrow early in 1804, and later was able to make ribald jokes to his friends about Mary's marriage to a fox-hunting squire, this romance was to haunt him for many years. One of the factors which enabled him to find some relief from it was a growing friendship with his half-sister Augusta, whom he met now for the first time. He made her his confidante, and was able to complain to her of his worsening relationship with his mother: 'The more I see of her the more my dislike augments,' he wrote. They quarrelled violently – she called him 'lame brat' – and he told Augusta: 'I have never been so *scurrilously*, and *violently* abused by any person, as by that woman, whom I think I am to call mother. . . . Within one little hour, I have not only heard myself, but have heard my *whole family*, by the father's side, *stigmatised* in terms that the *blackest malevolence* would perhaps shrink from. . . .'

Augusta

17

The Great Court and Chapel of Trinity College, Cambridge

This was in 1805, and Byron was already a radical and a nonconformist, beginning to rebel against religion, and rebelling also against school (where he led a miniature uprising against a new headmaster). In the summer he left Harrow, and in October took up residence in rooms in the south-east corner of the Great Court of Trinity College, Cambridge. His luggage included a new gown with gold embroidery, and one dozen bottles of port, sherry, claret and madeira.

His career at Cambridge was undistinguished: he drank, swam, rode and spent his money freely. Soon he was in the hands of the first of a long line of money-lenders, and his mother found that his bills for his first term came to twice what was expected. He bought a carriage, horses and harness, and ordered livery for his servants. There is no record of his attending a single lecture.

But it is from this time that his first serious poetry dates: in November 1806 a book of poems, *Fugitive Pieces*, appeared and (because of the mildly erotic nature of one of the poems) created the first characteristic scandal of his writing life. His answer to criticism was to collect up all but four copies, and burn them. Two *'Hours of* months later he produced a revised volume, *Hours of Idleness*, which sold fairly *Idleness'* well, and received one or two good reviews.

18

But his university life was lively rather than studious: he entertained his friends Charles Skinner Matthews and John Cam Hobhouse (the son of a Bristol M P, and one of his lifelong friends), got more and more deeply into debt, and alienated the authorities not only by more enthusiastic flirtations than most young men of his age, but by a contempt for rules and regulations – as when, annoyed by a statute forbidding him to keep a dog in his rooms, he bought a tame bear and kept it in college, intending that it 'should sit for a fellowship'.

Lord Byron at Cambridge. 'As might be supposed I like a College Life extremely, especially as I have escaped the Trammels or rather Fetters of my domestic Tyrant Mrs Byron. . . . I am now most pleasantly situated in *Super*excellent Rooms, flanked on one side by my Tutor, on the other by an old Fellow, both of whom are rather checks upon my *vivacity*.'

Suddenly, at Christmas 1807, he decided to leave Cambridge, and appeared in London at Dorant's Hotel, from which he launched into society with the greatest vigour and considerable injudiciousness: he over-published (*Poems Original and Translated* came out in March), slimmed until it made him ill, went to Brighton and bathed to excess, fell into over-dramatized melancholy, and began making the acquaintance of the professional ladies of the *ton* – the Fashionable Impure, as they were politely called – who displayed themselves in private boxes at the opera, or in their carriages in the park.

For the first time, but not the last, he kept a girl in his rooms disguised as a page, and at the same time started affairs with a number of other women – affairs in which, at the time at least, he was perfectly sincere, but in which he seemed to need to prove to himself that despite his club foot (which in fact was scarcely noticeable), despite the vulgarity of his childhood, he was desirable.

'BON TON': 'Pon honor Lady Caroline, You appear a divinity! – by Jove those Jewels are of the première qualité – did Love furnish them?'
'On my truth Sir William You are a gay Man.'

A fountain in the cloisters at Newstead. 'Lord Byron took a notion that there was a deal of money buried about the Abbey by the monks in old times, and nothing would serve him but he must have the flagging taken up in the cloisters. . . . Several of the skulls [found] were cleaned and put in frames in his room.' – Housekeeper at Newstead

His debts mounting now to over £12,000, he retired to Newstead, which he intended to make his home. He could ill afford it, but began to redecorate, engaged servants – including William Fletcher, who was to remain his valet until his death, and Robert Rushton, the handsome son of a local farmer, who was to accompany him on his first journey abroad. For he was thinking now of travelling, and suggested to Hanson that a six-month voyage to the East would scarcely cost more than £500 (though he would have to settle his debts, and should have perhaps £3,000 to carry with him in case of emergencies). Since the money was not available, he spent his time excavating the cloisters at Newstead, where he found a number of stone coffins full of bones. He had one coffin placed in the great hall, put several skulls in his room, and paid seventeen guineas to have one polished and set in silver as a drinking-cup.

Meanwhile, he was at work on his first considerable poem – a satire in verse prompted by the contemptuous review of *Hours of Idleness* which had appeared in the *Edinburgh Review*. In it, he set about the critics, laid into Southey, Scott, Wordsworth, Coleridge, and the other poets of the romantic school. But his main, and dangerous, target was the critics:

> *A man must serve his time to every trade*
> *Save censure – Critics all are ready-made . . .*
> *Fear not to lie, 'twill seem a sharper hit;*
> *Shrink not from blasphemy, 'twill pass for wit;*
> *Care not for feeling – pass your proper jest*
> *And stand a Critic, hated yet caress'd.*

The poem was written in high spirits, and was extremely successful. While he was writing it, he was also reading political works – in preparation for taking his seat in the House of Lords – and getting one of the Newstead maids with child. He also added to his debts with gifts to his friends – such as the breakfast-cup which he bought for £500, as a present for a new-born baby.

View of the House of Lords and Commons from Old Palace Yard

'The Glenarvon ghost at the masquerade.' An illustrations to the *Memoirs* of Harriette Wilson, the famous courtesan.

He took his seat in the Lords a few days before *English Bards and Scotch Reviewers* came out; and returned almost immediately to Newstead, where he gave a farewell party – for by now Hanson had promised him money for his voyage abroad. The countryside around Newstead resounded with rumours of an orgy at the Abbey. Although the party was innocent enough, Byron encouraged the rumours, hinting at amusements more adult than dressing up as a monk and hiding in a coffin. Later, he began the perpetuation of the legend when in the first canto of *Childe Harold* he described himself:

> *Ah me! in sooth he was a shameless wight,*
> *Sore given to revel and ungodly glee;*
> *Few earthly things found favour in his sight*
> *Save concubines and carnal companie,*
> *And flaunting wassailers of high and low degree.*

His talent for self-dramatization was very considerable.

'*English Bards and Scotch Reviewers*'

Byron and Robert Rushton
Where rose the mountains, there to him
were friends;
Where roll'd the ocean, thereon was his home;
Where a blue sky, and glowing clime, extends,
He had the passion and the power to roam....

In April, Byron met his friend Hobhouse in London and persuaded him to join the expedition abroad. He commissioned an artist to paint himself and Robert Rushton in a romantic pose beside a vaguely alien shore, and was encouraged on his way by the news that *English Bards* was going into a second edition. The friends coached to Falmouth, and on 2 July 1809 sailed on the Falmouth Packet for Lisbon, together with Fletcher, Rushton, and over £100 worth of books (including *Gulliver's Travels* and *Robinson Crusoe*). 'The world is all before me!' he wrote to his mother.

Byron's first tour abroad was of enormous importance: it was his introduction to Europe (he never lived contentedly in England again), and it provided the material for the autobiographical *Childe Harold's Pilgrimage*, the first of his two great picaresque novels in verse. The enthusiasm and delight with which he went ashore in Lisbon are reflected in the first of that wonderful series of letters he sent to his mother:

24

Falmouth Harbour *Now at last we're off for Turkey/Lord knows when we shall come back!*

Lisbon from Fort Almeida *What beauties doth Lisboa first unfold!*
Her image floating on that noble tide
Which poets vainly pave with sands of gold
But now whereon a thousand keels did ride
Of mighty strength. . . .

Mrs Byron. 'That parent who by her outrageous conduct forfeits all title to filial affection.'

Plaza San Francisco, Seville *Here Folly still his votaries inthrals;*
And young-eyed Lewdness walks her midnight rounds. . . .

'I am very happy here because I loves oranges, and talks bad Latin to the monks, who understand it, as it is like their own – and I goes into society (with my pocket pistols), and I swims in the Tagus all across at once, and I rides on an ass or a mule, and swears Portuguese. . . .'

These letters (the most high-spirited, witty and entertaining letters of any British poet) describe the adventures, real and imaginary, that he had on his way to Seville, and then, at the beginning of August, on to Gibraltar, Sardinia, Malta (where he flirted with the pretty wife of a local Governor, and almost fought a duel about her), Patras and Prevesa.

27

The Temple of Jupiter Olympus,
Athens
Here let me sit upon this massy stone,
The marble column's yet unshaken base;
Here, son of Saturn! was thy fav'rite throne:
Mightiest of many such! Hence let me trace
The latent grandeur of thy dwelling-place.

(*left*) Ali Pasha, late Vizier of Jannina
'He told me to consider him as a father
while I was in Turkey, and said he
looked on me as his son.'

(*opposite*) Byron in Albanian costume.
'I have some very "magnifiques"
Albanian dresses, the only expensive
articles in this country. They cost fifty
guineas each, and have so much gold,
they would cost in England
two hundred.'

28

Fitted out at Jannina with romantic Albanian costumes, Byron and Hobhouse made an expedition to Tepelene, where they were received by the murderous despot Ali Pasha, the absolute ruler of Albania, and were properly impressed by his mild appearance. In the autumn (after passing through Missolonghi, where Byron was to die in fifteen years' time) the travellers reached Athens, already conscious of the rising Greek hatred for Turkish dominion.

Greece   It was during this autumn, in Athens, that Byron's lifelong devotion to Greece really took root: appalled by Lord Elgin's despoliation of the Acropolis, he conceived a violent attack on him – and devoted the rest of his time to his landlady's three beautiful teen-age daughters, Mariana, Katinka and Theresa (the *Maid of Athens* of his poem), and to a handsome boy, Nicolo Giraud, who began to learn English from him.

In March there was another expedition – to Smyrna and the plains of Troy, and to Sestos (where Byron made his famous swim across the Hellespont to Abydos, in imitation of Leander). As he voyaged on up the Bosphorus to Constantinople, the filth and cruelty of the Turkish Empire appalled him. His first sight of the Sultan's palace at Constantinople was from the river. Two dogs nibbled at a dead body beneath its walls. Contempt for human life seemed complete: here the exposed heads of criminals, there the headless body of a recently executed man. His distaste for the Turks grew (although, later, he was to see public executions both in London and in Rome without comment on their morality).

The Maid of Athens
Though I fly to Istambol,
Athens holds my heart and soul:
Can I cease to love thee? No!

(*right above*) Smyrna from the Jews' Burial Ground

(*right below*) The Capuchin Convent, Athens

30

31

By now, he had been abroad for over a year; and when he returned to Athens, the news was a mixture of good and bad – *English Bards* was going into a third edition; but his debts were still outstanding. He decided to stay in Athens, and took rooms at a Capuchin convent there, with Nicolo as his servant and companion. Theresa Macri's mother had whisked her away from Byron's vicinity ('Can I cease to love thee? No!', he wrote); but there was a highly romantic incident when he intervened to save a Turkish girl condemned for unfaithfulness, who was about to be thrown into the sea in a sack – an incident he commemorated in his poem *The Giaour*. More seriously, he began to take an interest in Greek politics, and wrote several essays on the current situation, as well as on modern Greek language and literature.

Return to England But by April of 1811 he had decided to return to England. Hanson was threatening to sell Newstead to liquidate the bills, and this was to be prevented at all costs. He sailed from Athens on 22 April with Nicolo (whom he put to school in Malta), and came ashore at Sheerness on 14 July – two years and twelve days after he had sailed from Falmouth. He was more radical than ever; he had the manuscript of *Childe Harold* in his pocket; and a passion for Greece. 'If I am a poet,' he said, 'the air of Greece has made me one.'

Boatswain
*To mark a friend's remains
 these stones arise;
I never knew but one, – and
 here he lies.*

'Childe Harold's Pilgrimage' by J.M.W. Turner   . . . *the deep umbrage of a green hill's shade*
Which shows a distant prospect far away. . . .

But as he reached London, so did the news of the sudden death of his mother. He rushed on to Newstead, where he gave way to an excess of sentimental grief over the woman he had so cordially disliked. 'Oh, Mrs By!' he exclaimed to her maid, 'I had but one friend in the world, and she is gone!'

Almost on the day of his mother's funeral, he heard of the death of his friend Matthews; and then of that of a Harrow school friend, John Wingfield. In a mood of acute melancholy, Byron made his own will: he left £7,000 to Nicolo, £50 a year each to his servants, and instructed that his own body was to be buried in a vacant space left for it in a vault in the garden at Newstead where a favourite dog, Boatswain, had been interred. 'And it is my will', he said firmly, 'that my faithful dog may not be removed from the said vault.'

Gradually, however, his spirits revived. He discussed the publication of *Childe Harold* with his friends and John Murray, his publisher; and in February 1812,

33

Nottingham. 'We must not allow mankind to be sacrificed to improvements in mechanism.'

Holland House, where Byron met Lady Caroline Lamb

Henry Fox, 3rd Baron Holland.

William Lamb, later Lord Melbourne

made a fluent maiden speech in the House of Lords, in support of measures to alleviate the distress of the stocking weavers of Nottingham, who were then rioting under the pressures of the mechanization of their trade. On 10 March *Childe Harold* was published.

Everyone recognized the poem as autobiographical, however much the author himself denied the fact; and the wit and flashing narrative of the piece captivated its readers. Within three days, five hundred copies had been sold; the many libraries distributed the poem still further. Byron became an almost instant social success, receiving within a week the accolade of an invitation to Holland House, in Kensington, where Lord and Lady Holland held the most fashionable gatherings in London. There he met Lady Caroline Lamb, the beautiful and spirited wife of a rising politician, William Lamb (later Lord Melbourne). She 'longed to know Byron' – and was soon to know him all too well.

In a short time, it was common knowledge that Byron and Lady Caroline were having an affair; and even in a promiscuous age, that affair became scandalous. She was besotted by the handsome young poet, with his olive complexion, his

Fame

dark eyes. In her novel *Glenarvon* (which, after the affair had broken up, she wrote as an act of revenge) she described her first meeting with him:

'The eye beamed into life as it threw up its dark, ardent gaze, with a look nearly of inspiration, while the proud curl of the upper lip expressed haughtiness and bitter contempt; yet, even mixed with these fierce characteristic feelings, an air of melancholy and dejection shaded and softened every harsher expression. Such a countenance spoke to the heart, and filled it with one vague yet powerful interest – so strong, so indefinable, that it could not be easily overcome.'

Lady Caroline was passionately in love, outdoing every courtesan in London in the determination of her assaults on his time and his affection. Eventually he began to find her constant importunings boring, and refused her admission; she dressed herself as a page, arriving at his lodgings with a letter while he was entertaining a friend, Robert Charles Dallas. The page, Dallas noticed, 'was a fair-faced, delicate boy of thirteen or fourteen years old, whom one might have taken for the lady herself! . . . He had light hair curling about his face, and held a feathered hat in his hand which completed the effect of this urchin Pandarus. I could not but suspect at the time that it was a disguise. . . .'

Lady Caroline Lamb in page's costume. 'You know I have always thought you the cleverest, most agreeable, absurd, amiable, perplexing, dangerous, fascinating little being. . . . I won't talk to you of beauty; I am no judge. But our beauties cease to be so when near you.'

Lady Caroline Lamb on horseback. 'You talked to me about keeping her out. It is impossible; she comes at all times, at any time, and the moment the door is open in she walks. I can't throw her out of the window . . . I am already almost a prisoner; she has no shame, no feeling, no one estimable or redeemable quality.'

Despairing, as Byron's rejection became more obvious, Lady Caroline attempted to run away from home; but was recaptured by Byron himself and returned to her family. Her mother took her to Ireland, whence she continued to write adoring, pleading letters. Finally, losing all patience, he wrote her a final, cruel letter (which she published, in a heavily adapted form, in *Glenarvon*):

'Lady Caroline . . . were I inclined to reproach you I might for 20 thousand things, but I will not. They really are not cause of my present conduct – my opinion of you is entirely alter'd, & if I had wanted anything to confirm me, your Levities your caprices & the mean subterfuges you have lately made use of while madly gay – of writing to me as if otherwise, would entirely have open'd my eyes. I am no longer yr. lover – I shall but never be less than your friend.'

Gradually Lady Caroline overcame her hysteria and settled down to write her commemorative novel; and meanwhile, letters of passionate admiration poured in addressed to the author of *Childe Harold* from ladies all over the country – often accompanied by locks of hair and suggesting secret assignations. Byron's confidence in his own attractions was greatly increased.

Jane Elizabeth, Countess of Oxford

Lady Melbourne

Melbourne House, Whitehall

Byron aged twenty-five. He thought this 'the very best' portrait made of him, and approved of the artist, James Holmes, 'because he takes such inveterate likenesses'.

One pleasant result of his affair with Lady Caroline was that, oddly enough, it left him on friendly terms with her mother-in-law, the somewhat eccentric but extremely witty and attractive Lady Melbourne; and it was to her that Byron announced, quite suddenly, that he thought he would like to marry – and to marry William Lamb's cousin, a young blue-stocking of twenty, Annabella Milbanke (to whom, ironically enough, Lady Caroline had been the first to introduce him). When Lady Melbourne spoke to Annabella on the subject, the latter replied that she feared she could not feel a sufficiently 'strong attraction' to Lord Byron. This was enough to redouble his attentions to her: 'You may tell her', he wrote to Lady Melbourne, 'I am more proud of her *rejection* than I can ever be of *another's acceptance*.' At the same time he was writing consolingly to Lady Caroline in Ireland (genuinely repenting of his former curtness); conducting an affair with Lady Oxford (a beautiful but middle-aged lady with two handsome daughters); and moving in society – visiting, for instance, Princess Caroline at Kensington Palace, and meeting Madame de Staël.

Annabella Milbanke

39

'The Bride of Abydos', an illustration to the poem

He was becoming more and more notorious, better and better known. In July there was a scandalous scene at a party in London, when Lady Caroline, returned from Ireland, threatened to stab herself in Byron's presence. Fantastic stories circulated and abusive notes appeared in the scurrilous press. By now *The Giaour* had been published and was about to go into a second edition; and it was followed in December by *The Bride of Abydos*, the romantic story in verse of the love of an eastern beauty for her cousin, a pirate chief. The poem was written, Byron said, to take his mind off Lady Frances Webster, the wife of his friend James Wedderburn Webster.

'The Corsair'   In January yet another poem appeared: *The Corsair*, in which another obvious self-portrait drew the attention of the public – so much so that 10,000 copies of the poem were sold on the day of publication, and 25,000 copies within a month. The phenomenal sale had something to do with Byron's personal reputation, but much also to do with the strangeness of the characters and settings of his poems.

40

'High Life at Almack's'

Here were Maugrebins and Mamelukes, Caiques and Tophaiks, Yatagans and
Jereeds; and the notes to the poems were full of the most fascinating information –
how, when a Turk was in a passion, his beard curled; how an emir was distinguished by his green robe. And, of course, as the public immediately recognized,
Conrad, the pirate chief and hero of *The Corsair*, was the poet himself – Byron
by Byron:

> *That man of loneliness and mystery,*
> *Scarce seen to smile, and seldom heard to sigh . . .*
>
> *Though smooth his voice, and calm his general mien*
> *Still seems there something he would not have seen . . .*
>
> *As if within that murkiness of mind*
> *Worked feelings fearful, and yet undefined. . . .*

41

Annabella Milbanke aged twenty.
'Miss Milbanke was not without a
certain amount of prettiness or
cleverness; but her manner was stiff and
formal, and gave one the idea of being
self-willed and self-opinionated. She
was almost the only young, pretty,
well-dressed girl we ever saw who
carried no cheerfulness along with her.'
– The Rev. Mr Harness

During this winter, it is clear that Byron was under enormous psychological
pressure: he ground his teeth in his sleep so savagely that he was forced to consult
a dentist, and to the tensions of the frenetic social life he was living, were added
financial difficulties (which he did little to abate: he had given the copyright of
The Corsair, for which the publisher paid 1,000 guineas, to his friend Dallas, and
gave his half-sister Augusta £3,000 to help clear the gambling debts of her Army
husband, Colonel Leigh). He had been attempting to negotiate the sale of
Newstead, but the arrangement had fallen through. Meanwhile, the mysterious
relationship between him and his half-sister, which has attracted so much
speculation, was evidently causing him considerable anxiety, pursued still as he
was by his childhood Calvinist sense of guilt.

Augusta pressed him to marry; and at the beginning of 1814 he wrote to
Annabella Milbanke, with whom he had been carrying on a desultory correspondence since that first hint of a proposal through Lady Melbourne.

Newstead, *c.* 1828

'I did – do – and always shall love you', he wrote. But Annabella remained cool, and by August Byron was back at Newstead, writing a little and trying to fight boredom by shooting the tops off soda-water bottles in the grounds. On 9 September he proposed to Annabella again; this time she accepted. As he was reading her letter, the Newstead gardener came into the room – he had just uncovered in the garden Byron's mother's wedding ring, which she had lost some years before. On 2 January 1815 he was to place it on Annabella's finger.

The whole affair was a desperately difficult one for both Byron and his fiancée. His biographers have speculated endlessly about the marriage and the precise reasons why it was so disastrous. She was a prude, she was over-sensitive, she was a blue-stocking and a spoilt and naïve child. He was insensitive, brutal, unfaithful, sensual and coarse. The accusations mount; and there is some truth in most of them. But the basic truth is that they were incompatible on almost every ground. Yet there is no doubt that there was goodwill on both sides: 'I must, of course, reform thoroughly', Byron wrote to Tom Moore; 'She is so good a person that – that – in short, I wish I were a better.'

Judith Milbanke, 1784   Ralph Milbanke, 1778

Seaham harbour. 'Upon this dreary coast, we have nothing but county meetings and shipwrecks:
And I have this day dined upon fish, which probably dined upon the crews of
several colliers lost in the late gales.'

Byron aged twenty-six. 'There can be no doubt that Byron was a little maddish' – The Rev. Mr Harkness

'He is a person of the most consummate genius, and capable, if he would direct his energies to such an end, of becoming the redeemer of his country. But it is his weakness to be proud.' – Shelley

Their first meeting after their engagement was an embarrassing one. He set out to charm her parents, Sir Ralph and Lady Milbanke, and succeeded brilliantly; but Annabella herself simply made him feel uncomfortable. 'She is the most *silent* woman I ever encountered; which perplexes me extremely', he wrote to Lady Melbourne. Byron's temper was not improved by the knowledge that he might have to sell Newstead in order to provide a proper marriage settlement; and it seemed for a while that the engagement might be broken off. But it was not, and Byron returned to London to prepare for his wedding. In the meantime, he embarked upon an affair with Eliza Francis, a young poetess who had called upon him to beg a subscription for her own poems. Immediately after Christmas he travelled north to the Milbankes' home at Seaham, County Durham. There, in the drawing-room, he and Annabella were married.

Halnaby Hall. 'We were married yesterday at ten upon ye clock, so there's an end of that matter. . . . All those who are disposed to make presents may as well send them forthwith, and pray let them be handsome.'

Marriage   Lady Milbanke was by now less sanguine. Marriage to the sixth Baron Byron did not seem likely to have even the anticipated advantages for her daughter. 'Never before or *since* Marriage has he made any present to Lady B., not even the *common one* of a diamond hoop ring', she complained. At midday the church bells rang, a few enthusiasts fired muskets at the door of the house at Seaham, and Lord and Lady Byron set out by coach for Halnaby Hall, forty miles away, where they were to spend their honeymoon.

It was an uncomfortable ride, though the precise truth about it is obscured by the accusations and counter-accusations of later years. Annabella's complaints of her husband's over-precipitate coarseness may or may not have been true; but whatever the facts about the journey, it is certainly true that the honeymoon itself was not a success. Certainly they read together, invented affectionate nicknames for each other, and she copied out several of the *Hebrew Melodies* on which he was working; but the atmosphere was gloomy. Byron himself set the mood when, coming down to breakfast on the morning after his wedding day, he stared unhappily out across the snow-laden park, and said: 'It is too late now. It is done and cannot be undone.'

46

Thomas Moore
What are you doing now,
  Oh Thomas Moore?
What are you doing now,
  Oh Thomas Moore?
Sighing or suing now,
Rhyming or wooing now,
Billing or cooing now,
Which, Thomas Moore?

Byron commonly melodramatized everything; Annabella, naïve and un-
sophisticated, believed everything he said. She spoke later of his uncertain temper,
his nightmares, his mysterious hints of dreadful incidents in his past. She even
alleged that he had told her of his attempts to seduce a twelve-year-old child; and
she believed him! He was, she said, over-sensitive about his 'little foot', and at the
same time proud and vain.

Yet there were moments when they believed themselves happy. From Seaham,
where they travelled at the end of January, and where Byron spent his twenty-
seventh birthday, he wrote to Tom Moore: 'I still think one ought to marry upon
lease; but am very sure I should renew mine at the expiration, though the next
term were for ninety and nine years.'

The entrance to Newmarket

Despite the precarious nature of their daughter's happiness, which must surely have been evident to them, Sir Ralph and Lady Milbanke were hospitable and showed every sign of accepting Byron as a son. But he was unbearably bored at Seaham, and on 9 March travelled to Newmarket with Annabella, on a visit to Augusta at her home in Six Mile Bottom. At Seaham he had told Annabella: 'I think I love you', and: 'You do make me happy'; at Six Mile Bottom he took to staying up with Augusta night after night, after Annabella had been dismissed to bed with a curt: 'We don't want *you*, my charmer!' He and Augusta exchanged gold lockets with pieces of each other's hair – and although, drinking heavily, he quarrelled with Augusta as well as with his wife, the former had learned how to manage him.

◀ Augusta Leigh

49

Piccadilly from Hyde Park Turnpike, with Piccadilly Terrace on the left

In the middle of March, he took Annabella on to London. Though his debts now mounted to over £30,000, he rented the Duchess of Devonshire's house at 13 Piccadilly Terrace – a fatal step, for his creditors saw him apparently preparing to plunge into the immensely extravagant social life of London. This was perhaps more openly extravagant than it ever had been, or ever would be again. Lord Alvanley was able to spend £150 on strawberries alone, for one of his famous breakfasts; Beau Brummell (whose importance Byron rated above that of Napoleon!) alleged that his boot-blacking was made from the finest champagne; Lord Grey remarked that he would not dress Lady Londonderry for under £5,000 a year, for her handkerchiefs cost fifty guineas a dozen. The bucks and swells ruled the fashionable world, politely late for every appointment, gambling prodigiously and dressing richly – and sharing their world with the great ladies who moved with such elegance through the bright ballrooms of Mayfair, where, one contemporary wrote, the noise of carriage wheels was like the fall of Niagara from six to eight, from ten till midnight.

No wonder that the tradesmen and money-lenders to whom Byron was indebted, seeing him living in this society, began to worry him for repayment.

50

George ('Beau') Brummell.
'The mob would gather every
morning round his door to see him
descend, insolent from his toilet, and
mount and ride away.'

The Dandy Club, 1818.
'I was a member, at the time too of
its greatest glory, when Brummell
and Mildmay, Alvanley and
Pierrepoint, gave the Dandy Balls;
and we got up the famous
masquerade at Burlington House
and Garden, for Wellington. . . .'

Notice of the sale of Newstead Abbey by auction.
'From the moment of the useless effort to sell Newstead and other estates, Lord Byron's difficulties began to increase.' – Hobhouse

(*right above*) 'Lobby Loungers', taken from the saloon of Drury Lane Theatre. By I. R. Cruikshank

(*right below*) 'A Buz in a Box, or the Poet in a Pet': the opening of the New Drury Lane Theatre, 1812

'Hebrew Melodies'

Hebrew Melodies, a collection of short poems set by Isaac Nathan to favourite airs sung in the religious services of the Jews, was published in April at the extravagant price of one guinea (at that time, a short poem generally sold at 6s. 6d., and a three-volume novel at between 12s. and 18s.). Despite this, 10,000 copies of the book were sold. The poems are not outstanding – though the book did include one of Byron's best-known and best-loved lyrics, *She Walks in Beauty.*

Although Byron seemed to his friends to be happy enough, he was still under enormous strain. He suffered from insomnia and irrational fears, walked about the house at night, constantly carried pistols against some quite imaginary danger. Annabella was pregnant, and he was irritable with her and even with Augusta; his creditors continued to press him. He was forced to take the final step and put Newstead up for sale: but the house and estate was bought in at 95,000 guineas – 75,000 guineas had been offered, but Byron considered the sum insufficient to meet all his debts.

By November a bailiff had camped in the house in Piccadilly Terrace, and
Byron was driven out of doors by this and by Annabella's refusal to bear with his
ill-temper. She took him, as usual, over-seriously. Fletcher, his valet, said: 'It is
very odd, but I never knew a lady that could not manage my lord, *except* my lady.'
Desperately, Annabella sent for Augusta and appealed to her to placate Byron,
who seemed every day to fly into a new drunken rage, and was spending more and
more of his time at the Drury Lane Theatre (where he had been appointed to the
sub-committee of management, and had 'taken up' a young actress, Susan Boyce).

Byron later admitted that, irritated by his financial difficulties and by the confusion into which the house had been thrown by the arrival of a baby (for *Birth of Ada* Augusta Ada Byron had been born on 10 December 1815), he had treated Annabella unkindly.

'One day in the middle of my [financial] trouble I came into the room, and went up to the fire; she was standing before it, and said "Am I in your way?" I answered "Yes, you *are*", with emphasis. She burst into tears, and left the room. I hopped upstairs as quickly as I could and begged her pardon MOST humbly; and that was the only time I spoke really harshly to her.'

Under this kind of provocation, Annabella eventually became frantic. After a bitter argument she decided she would leave London. Searching Byron's room, she had found a small bottle of laudanum; taking it to a doctor, she inquired whether it was possible that he might be certifiably insane. She also began speaking to some of his friends on the same assumption. Word soon reached Byron, who was aghast and angry. He was later to write of the incident in *Don Juan*, the first canto of which contains an unflattering portrait of Lady Byron:

> *For Inez called some druggists and physicians,*
> *And tried to prove her loving lord was mad,*
> *But as he had some lucid intermissions,*
> *She next decided he was only* bad.

(*left below*) 'Fashionables of 1816', by I. R. Cruikshank. Byron, with the actress Mrs Mardyn on one arm and an unnamed beauty on the other, dominates the gathering.

Kirkby Mallory Hall. 'What day of January was it, when Lady B. marched upon Kirkby? which was the Signal of war.'

On 13 January Annabella prepared to travel to Kirkby Mallory in Leicestershire, to join her parents. She went to Byron, and offered him her hand. According to one biographer, he put his hands behind him and said: 'When shall we three meet again?' 'In Heaven, I trust', replied Annabella, and left. They never saw each other again.

Byron appears to have believed that the separation would only be temporary; but Lady Noel (Annabella's parents had changed their name to Noel, in compliance with the conditions of a legacy) made her daughter promise never to see her husband again, and began going from lawyer to lawyer, eventually finding one who was persuaded to write to Byron stating coldly: 'It cannot tend to your happiness to continue to live with Lady Byron', and inviting him to appoint 'a professional friend' to consider the terms of a permanent separation.

He was appalled and hurt; there had never been any *real* disagreements, he told Sir Ralph, and wrote to Annabella telling her that he would believe nothing until he heard from her: 'I loved you, and will not part from you without your express and expressed refusal to return to, or receive me.' But the position went from bad to worse: although Annabella was still drawn to Byron, although she believed him to be basically sincere, although Augusta was working for a reconciliation, rumours began to circulate, and under pressure from her parents Annabella handed her lawyers 'evidence of gross indecency in language and conduct'. Byron had officially refused a separation; she must take him to court.

Separation

55

William Godwin
. . . ye make the Rights of Man your theme,
Your Country libel, and your God blaspheme.

Claire Clairmont.
'To express it delicately, I think Madame
Claire is a damned bitch.'

Claire Clairmont   And in the midst of such a passionate upheaval in his private life, yet another
fateful meeting occurred. Byron received a packet of poems from a seventeen-year-
old girl. It was followed by letter after admiring letter; and then by personal calls.
Finally Byron admitted her. She was the step-daughter of the radical philosopher
William Godwin, and had been living with her step-sister Mary Godwin, who
herself had left her husband in order to live with the poet Shelley. The girl's name
was Mary Jane Clairmont. Byron preferred to call her Claire.

He at last signed a preliminary agreement for a separation and with it sent
Annabella a set of verses:

> Fare thee well! and if for ever,
> Still for ever, fare thee well. . . .

The poem is, or appears, passionately sincere; but a Tory paper, the *Champion*,
somehow got hold of a copy and printed it. The outcry was immediate and
considerable. Wordsworth joined it, perhaps not entirely because of Byron's
attack on him in *English Bards*: 'Let me say only one word of Lord B. The man
is insane. . . . The wretched verses are disgusting in sentiment, and in execution
contemptible. "Though my many faults deface me" etc. Can worse doggerel
than such a stanza be written? One verse is commendable: "All my madness
none can know." ' It is clear that this was moral rather than poetical criticism.

'The Separation' by I. R. Cruikshank

'Fare Thee Well' by I. R. Cruikshank.

'I was abused in the public prints, made the common talk of private companies, hissed as I went to the house of Lords.'

Augusta Leigh, 1817

Still oppressed with debts, and with the problems of the separation, Byron planned to leave England. He sold his books (for a total of £723 12s. 6d.), and had a huge travelling coach built, with a library, a plate chest, and 'every apparatus for dining'. Concerned by the many rumours which were circulating about him, Augusta came to London to see her half-brother. It was their last meeting, and he gave her a poem:

> *When fortune changed – and Love fled far,*
> *And Hatred's shafts flew thick and fast,*
> *Thou wert the solitary star*
> *Which rose and set not to the last.*

On 21 April he signed the deed of separation, and two days later left London with the faithful Fletcher, Robert Rushton, another servant, and a young doctor, John William Polidori. They shut the door of the house in Piccadilly Terrace at 9.30 in the morning. Five minutes later the bailiffs forced entry and seized everything. At Dover, the news that Byron was in town collected a crowd around his hotel; ladies dressed as servant girls in order to get close to him. On 24 April he left England for the last time.

Dover Harbour.
'I ran to the end of the rough
wooden pier – and as the vessel
toss'd by as through a rough sea
saw him again – the dear fellow
pulled off his cap & wav'd it to me.
. . . God bless him for a gallant
spirit and a kind one.' – Hobhouse

Hôtel de Ville, Brussels

He certainly exaggerated the degree of public feeling against him, alleging that he had been insulted in the streets and hissed as he went to the House of Lords. But the press *was* full of rumours, and some newspapers had compared him to Nero, Caligula, Heliogabalus and Henry VIII. He felt his position acutely, and his relief at reaching Europe was enormous, although he showed no immediate signs of moral regeneration. Polidori wrote in his journal at Ostend: 'As soon as he reached his room, Lord B. fell like a thunderbolt upon the chambermaid.'

Waterloo Comfortable in his great coach, Byron rode on to Ghent, Antwerp and Brussels – and in the evening, toured with Polidori the field of Waterloo. That same night, he was asked to write in a lady's album, in which Sir Walter Scott had inscribed some lines on Waterloo. Byron took it, and returned it next day with two stanzas which later took their place in the new cantos he was to add to *Childe Harold*. They are among his most noble lines:

> *Stop! – for thy tread is on an Empire's dust!*
> *An Earthquake's spoil is sepulchred below!*
> *Is the spot mark'd with no colossal bust?*
> *Nor column trophied for triumphal show?*
> *None; but the moral's truth tells simpler so,*
> *As the ground was before, thus let it be; –*
> *How that red rain hath made the harvest grow!*
> *And is this all the world has gain'd by thee,*
> *Thou first and last of fields! king-making Victory?*

60

(*left*) The Duke of Wellington's headquarters at Waterloo

(*below*) Cologne

Byron aged twenty-eight

Leaving Brussels, Byron and his party travelled on to Cologne, where Byron had the first of many brushes with the egoistical Polidori. As the poet was reading one day, the young doctor suddenly turned to him and asked: 'And, pray, what is there excepting poetry that I cannot do better than you?'

'First', replied Byron, 'I can hit with a pistol the keyhole of that door; – Secondly, I can swim across that river to yonder point; – and Thirdly, I can give you a damned good thrashing.' Polidori's reply is not recorded.

A view of Clarens on Lake Geneva

The Villa Diodati

Dr J. W. Polidori.
'Very young and
hot-headed, and more
likely to incur diseases
than to cure them.'

By 24 May the party had reached Lausanne; and next day, Byron signed his name in the visitors' book of Dejean's Hôtel d'Angleterre near Geneva. He set down his age as one hundred.

Meanwhile, Shelley, with Mary Godwin and Claire Clairmont (carrying Byron's child, although no one but she knew of it), had left London for Switzerland. Claire had already suggested to Byron that they should all meet at Geneva. On 26 May Byron met Shelley for the first time on the shores of the lake there. They instantly took to each other; made a habit of breakfasting together every morning and house-hunting during the day. Early in June, Byron found the Villa Diodati – a handsome house two hundred yards from the lake, with a magnificent view of the Juras. Shelley settled near by, at Montalègre.

As usual, Byron was no sooner settled than he became unsettled. While he enjoyed his talks with Shelley, he found Polidori more and more irritating (indeed, the young doctor was already showing signs of that imbalance which resulted, later, in his suicide); and he found Claire's pressing attentions embarrassing – although he did not hesitate to take advantage of them. He was spied upon by the local people, and visiting English tourists insisted on calling.

63

Château de Chillon   *Lake Leman lies by Chillon's walls:*
A thousand feet in depth below
Its massy waters meet and flow. . . .

Chillon   Towards the end of June, he and Shelley set off along the lake to tour those places associated with Rousseau, whom they both admired. They called briefly at the forbidding Castle of Chillon, where Byron heard the story of the prisoner François Bonivard, which he set down later in a poem. Shelley seemed fascinated by the lake, and sailing on it. Even a violent storm, in which both poets almost drowned, did not disconcert him.

'He can't swim', Byron told John Murray. 'I stripped off my coat – made him strip off his and take hold of an oar, telling him that I thought (being myself an expert swimmer) I could save him, if he would not struggle when I took hold of him – unless we got smashed against the rocks, which were high and sharp, with an awkward surf on them at that minute. We were then about a hundred yards from shore, and the boat in peril. He answered me with the greatest coolness, that "he had no notion of being saved, and that I would have enough to do to save myself, and begged not to trouble me."'

64

Shelley. 'The least selfish and the mildest of men.'

Madame de Staël. 'Writes octavos and *talks* folios.'

Returning from the brief tour of the lake, Byron found Claire more and more importunate, and he became more and more impatient. It was a relief when Shelley and Mary took her off for a tour to Chamouni, leaving Byron to reacquaint himself with Madame de Staël (whose château was at Coppet, nearby), to write, and to worry about the rumours that were coming from England – where Annabella was driving Augusta frantic in her attempts to ensure that his step-sister never wrote to, or saw, Byron again; and where sets of spurious verses were being issued in his name.

By the time Shelley returned with the two women on 27 July, he had obviously learned of Claire's pregnancy, and Byron's position became embarrassing. He attempted to persuade Claire to promise to send the child to Augusta's care, but eventually yielded to her pressure and promised to look after his son or daughter. On 29 August Shelley and the women left for England – taking with them the manuscript of Canto III of *Childe Harold*, with *The Prisoner of Chillon* and some other poems. It was another permanent parting: although they were often to be in the same city, Claire was never to see Byron again.

Augusta had heard rumours of an affair; in a letter to her Byron (conveniently ignoring the fact that his child had been conceived in London) made a very typical excuse: 'As to all these "mistresses" – Lord help me – I have had but one. Now don't scold – but what could I do? A foolish girl, in spite of all I could say or do, would come after me, or rather went before for I found her here, and I have had all the plague possible to persuade her to go back again, but at last she went. Now dearest, I do most truly tell thee that I could not help this, that I did all I could to prevent it, and have at last put an end to it. I was not in love, nor have any love left for any; but I could not exactly play the Stoic with a woman who had scrambled eight hundred miles to unphilosophise me.'

The truth was that a pretty woman could always turn Byron's head. Conditioned in his childhood to think of himself, with his 'little foot', as a cripple, with a vulgar and ill-tempered mother whose qualities might also reside in him, he was quite incapable of refusing any woman whose attentions to him confirmed him attractive and lovable. And, of course, he was as inclined to loose living as any other man in a loose age.

67

The relaxation of moral standards, which had gradually been coming about during the illness of George III and the growing influence of the Prince of Wales, did not encourage self-restraint. 'The vices are wonderfully prolific among Whigs', wrote Miss Pamela Fitzgerald in 1816, 'and there are countless illegitimates – such a tribe of children of the mist. . . .' Indeed, the many children of the Countess of Oxford were known as the Harleian Miscellany because they were all assumed to have different fathers.

The men followed their inclinations without the faintest regard for the convenience or feelings of anyone but themselves. Lord Barrymore, driving home from a party in his phaeton, would crack half the windows on either side of the street with his whip. It was a great joke to throw a drunk into a pond, to rob a blind man of his dog, to swear freely and spit with the greatest force and accuracy. Women of any social order were fair game; and Byron simply followed the fashion when he found it quite unexceptionable to joke with Lady Melbourne about the indiscretions of her daughter-in-law.

The comparative poverty of his childhood, however, may have prevented him from the more disgusting vices of his time. Physical violence, unprovoked, did not attract him (although he admired, like everyone else, the professional bruisers

A cartoon by George Cruikshank

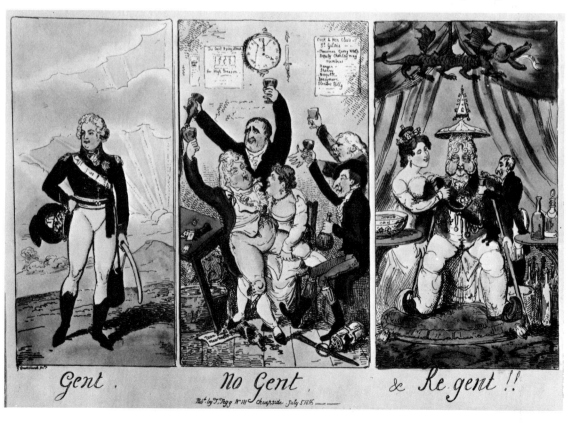

Gent.   No Gent.   & Re gent!!

La Scala, Milan. 'All society in Milan is carried on at the opera: they have private boxes where they play at cards, or talk, or anything else.'

on whose prowess he wagered). He did not think it funny to abuse the poor – as his speech in the Lords in defence of the Nottingham weavers had shown. But he could scarcely be completely free of the tendency of the age.

In September 1816, Hobhouse arrived in Switzerland, and the two men toured the mountains together. Byron started writing *Manfred*, the dramatic poem in which an outcast from society lives, tortured by remorse, among the mountains, seeking oblivion. In October they left the Villa Diodati for Milan. Byron had no special idea of his destination: he had a vague thought of travelling to Greece or Dalmatia – but first, he thought, he would see Venice.

En route, they passed through Milan, where they were introduced to Henri Beyle (Stendhal), who found Byron dandified, and thought he paid undue attention to his figure – but noted in his memoirs that when the talk turned to literary matters, 'his thoughts flowed with greater rapidity than his words, and his expressions were free from all affection or studied grace.'

69

Byron and Marianna Segati.
'She is by far the prettiest woman I
have seen here, and the most loveable I
have met with any where – as well as
one of the most singular.'

Venice Byron fell in love with Venice the moment he saw the city. He wrote to Tom
Moore: 'It is my intention to remain at Venice during the winter, probably, as it
has always been (next to the East) the greenest island of my imagination. It has
not disappointed me; though its evident decay would, perhaps, have that effect
upon others. But I have been familiar with ruins too long to dislike desolation.
Besides, I have fallen in love. . . . I have got some extremely good apartments in
the house of a "Merchant of Venice", who is a good deal occupied with business,
and has a wife in her twenty-second year.'

The landlord was a draper; his wife was called Marianna; the lodging in the
Frezzeria, off the Piazza San Marco. Made happy by the news that in London
John Murray had sold 7,000 copies each of Canto III of *Childe Harold* and *Chillon
and Other Poems* (for which he had been paid £2,000), Byron found his way into
Venetian society, rode, romanced, and began studying Armenian at the monastery
on San Lazzaro. He was, in fact, 'studious in the day and dissolute in the evening',
as he told Hobhouse.

In January, during the Carnival, he finished *Manfred*, and sent it off to Murray.
It was, he said, 'of a very wild, metaphysical and inexplicable kind . . . but I have

70

The Armenian monastery, San Lazzaro, near Venice

The Colleoni Statue, Venice, by James Holland

Carnival in Venice

Birth of Allegra at least rendered it *quite impossible* for the stage, for which my intercourse with D[rury] Lane has given me the greatest contempt.' On 12 January, in England, Claire had given birth to a daughter. The news came just as, satiated by the excitements and pleasures of the Carnival season, he had fallen ill with a fever. From his sick-bed he wrote his finest single lyric poem:

> So we'll go no more a roving
>   So late into the night,
> Though the heart be still as loving,
>   And the moon be still as bright.
>
> For the Sword outwears its sheath,
>   And the soul outwears the breast,
> And the heart must pause to breathe,
>   And Love itself have rest.

72

An execution in Rome, 1820. 'The day before I left Rome I saw three robbers guillotined. . . . The first turned me quite hot and thirsty, and made me shake so that I could hardly hold the opera-glass.' (*right*) The Bridge of Sighs, Venice

Nursed devotedly by the draper's wife, he recovered from his fever, and early in April left Venice for Rome, where he spent three weeks, noting down the impressions which he set into verse in the fourth canto of *Childe Harold*. As he walked on the roof of St Peter's, it is recorded, he was recognized by a group of English tourists. Lady Liddell, one of them, sternly told her daughter: 'Don't look at him; he is dangerous to look at!'

Deciding to live outside Venice during the summer, Byron took a lease on the Villa Foscarini, on the Brenta River at La Mira, seven miles upstream from the lagoon. There he settled down to work on the fourth canto of *Childe Harold*, and had soon sent off to Murray the first stanza with its description of Venice:

> *I stood in Venice, on the Bridge of Sighs;*
> *A palace and a prison on each hand:*
> *I saw from out the wave her structures rise*
> *As from the stroke of the enchanter's wand:*
> *A thousand years their cloudy wings expand*
> *Around me, and a dying Glory smiles*
> *O'er the far times, when many a subject land*
> *Look'd to the winged Lion's marble piles,*
> *Where Venice sate in state, throned on her hundred isles!*

Margarita Cogni.
'A very tall and formidable Girl of three and twenty, with the large black eyes and handsome face of a pretty fiend, a correspondent figure and a carriage as haughty as a Princess. . . .'

During the summer at La Mira, Byron met Margarita Cogni, the wife of a local baker, and began an affair with her; he was happy and relaxed, and after he had finished the first draft of Canto IV of *Childe Harold*, began another poem, *Beppo*, in which he tells an anecdote of a deceived Venetian husband. It is an ironic, witty piece – incidentally a revealing sketch of nineteenth-century Venetian life and morals – very much in the tone of Byron's letters, and in it he relaxed and expanded his poetic style: one can see in it the first signs of the discursive new style of *Don Juan*:

> *With all its sinful doings, I must say,*
>   *That Italy's a pleasant place to me,*
> *Who love to see the Sun shine every day,*
>   *And vines (not nail'd to walls) from tree to tree*
> *Festoon'd, much like the back scene of a play. . . .*

When he returned from La Mira to Venice in November 1817, Byron was able to set about clearing up his outstanding debts. Newstead had finally been sold for £94,500. He paid, at last, the £500 he owed for his travelling coach; he paid the six months' arrears of rent for the house in Piccadilly Terrace; and he planned to send to England for his daughter, who on 9 March of the next year was taken to St Giles-in-the-Fields in London, with Shelley's own two babies, and christened. In the register was written: 'Clara Allegra Byron, born of the Rt. Hon. George Gordon Lord Byron, ye reported father by Clara Mary Jane Clairmont.'

The Villa Foscarini, La Mira

Allegra. 'She is very pretty,
remarkably intelligent, and a great
favourite with everybody . . . she
has very blue eyes, and that
singular forehead, fair curly hair,
and a devil of a Spirit –
but that is Papa's.'

75

Byron in the
Palazzo Mocenigo

Immediately after the christening, the Shelleys set out for Italy, and by 4 April were in Milan. Byron, by now installed in the Palazzo Mocenigo, within sight of the Rialto, refused to communicate directly with Claire, and declined to *fetch* Allegra – so a Swiss nurse brought her to Venice.

In England, *Beppo* was published anonymously. It caused some scandal; but there were good reviews also, and Byron's authorship was generally known. Canto IV of *Childe Harold* came out in April, and was enthusiastically greeted by Sir Walter Scott, among other reviewers.

'Don Juan' begun

Byron's life in Venice during the summer months was one of almost frantic activity, both physical and mental. He began his masterpiece, *Don Juan*, with the farcical portrait of Lady Byron (as Donna Inez); and at the same time rode, romanced, swam. Swimming continued to be his most engrossing recreation. He was incapable of resisting a challenge; indeed in June he raced an ex-soldier of Napoleon, the Cavalier Angelo Mengaldo, from the Lido to the entrance to the Grand Canal, and won by five hundred yards after over four hours in the water.

Rumours about the style of his life found their way back to England: some of them true. His Palazzo was staffed by fourteen servants, presided over by Fletcher, who never tired of grumbling about Italy, the Italians, the food and the weather. In the Palazzo there were also two monkeys, a fox and two mastiffs. Byron himself seemed to cultivate eccentricity. He had been seen, leaving a party, to throw himself into the canal fully dressed, and to strike out for his Palazzo, swimming with one hand, and in the other holding a lantern to warn approaching gondoliers.

76

The Venetian Lagoon, by Guardi

The Rialto, by J. M. W. Turner

English visitors carried home with them distressing stories of his condition, of 'a fat, fat-headed, middle-aged man, slovenly to the extreme, unkempt, with long, untied locks that hung down on his shoulders, shabbily dressed. . . .'

Some of these rumours brought the Shelleys and Claire to Venice in August 1818, Claire not unnaturally worried about Allegra. Her presence in the city was kept a secret from Byron, and Shelley seemed to have little effect upon Byron's way of life – although they rediscovered the pleasure they had found, in Switzerland, in each other's company, and delighted in riding and talking together. Shelley commemorated one such ride in his *Julian and Maddalo*:

> *So, as we rode, we talked; and the swift thought,*
> *Winging itself with laughter, lingered not,*
> *But flew from brain to brain, – such glee was ours. . . .*

But Shelley was not blind to Byron's faults:

> *The sense that he was greater than his kind*
> *Had struck, methinks, his eagle spirit blind*
> *By gazing on its own exceeding light.*

78

'A Noble Poet
scratching up His Ideas'

Byron in Venice

In November, Hanson arrived in Venice for a holiday. His son was shocked to find the celebrated poet looking nearer to forty than thirty years of age. He wrote in his journal: 'His face had become pale, bloated and sallow. He had grown very fat, his shoulders broad and round, and the knuckles of his hands were lost in fat.' It is an unattractive portrait, but there is no reason to doubt Newton Hanson's word; this was the most dissipated year of Byron's life, and it fatally weakened him.

His work, however, was not suffering; he was writing, indeed, more fluently than ever. He had sent the first canto of *Don Juan* back to England, where Hobhouse had been aghast at its improprieties. He wrote in his diary: 'The blasphemies and facetiae and the domestica facta overpower even the great genius it displays.' It could never possibly be published, he told Byron; and Byron at first tended to agree, insisting only that a few copies should be privately printed for his personal use. But gradually he became more and more convinced that it should be issued, though anonymously – and, moreover, without any of the many cuts Hobhouse and some other friends suggested.

The life he was leading began to tell on him. He was beginning to feel, if not old, then middle-aged:

> But now at thirty years my hair is grey –
>   (I wonder what it will be like at forty?
> I thought of a peruke the other day –)
>   My heart is not much greener; and, in short, I
> Have squandered my whole summer while 'twas May. . . .

79

Teresa Guiccioli aged eighteen. 'She is pretty, a great coquette, extremely vain, excessively affected, clever enough, without the smallest principle, with a good deal of imagination and some passion.'

Teresa Guiccioli But in April came his meeting with the woman who was to bring him as much domestic happiness as he achieved in his life. She was a beautiful nineteen-year-old girl, married to the twice-widowed fifty-eight-year-old Count Alessandro Guiccioli. Teresa was introduced to Byron at an evening party; they talked of Dante and Petrarch and of Ravenna, her home. Byron was enchanted: and so, evidently, was Teresa, for the couple began soon to meet secretly – but not so secretly that the Venetians did not notice. Gossip started.

One evening, as Byron was in his box at the theatre listening to a performance of Rossini's *Otello*, Teresa – defying all custom – ran in to tell him that her husband had decided to return to Ravenna in the morning. As soon as she had left, he realized that he was truly in love with her. He wrote her long letters in studiously romantic Italian:

'You shall be my last Passion. I may well hope not to fall in love again, now that everything has become indifferent to me. Before I knew you – I felt an interest in many women, but never in one only. Now I love *you*, there is no other woman in the world for me.'

By June he had decided to go to her, and Count Guiccioli, apparently unsuspecting, invited him to call the moment he arrived in Ravenna. He did so; and soon was in the throes of a complicated affair which he was convinced would be his last. He wrote to Wedderburn Webster:

Palazzo Guiccioli, Ravenna

The set for *Otello* at La Scala,
designed by Alessandro Sanguirico

'My hair is half grey, and the Crow's-foot has been rather lavish of its indelible steps. My hair, though not gone, seems going, and my teeth remain by way of courtesy; but I suppose they will follow, having been too good to last.'

However, he settled down to a relatively untroubled romance – which was disturbed in July by the Count. Guiccioli must by now have known that he was being cuckolded, and felt unable to ignore the positive hints of an anonymous squib in verse which was sent to him. On 9 August he took Teresa off with him on a visit to his property at Bologna. Byron followed, and the Count – perhaps because he had found Byron willing to use his influence to have him made Consul or Vice-Consul for Ravenna – remained friendly. He even encouraged the poet to continue his friendship with Teresa. Byron was indeed devoted; when Teresa was away with her husband, he took her copy of Mme de Staël's *Corinne*, and wrote on the index-page (in English, which he knew she could not read): 'You will recognise the handwriting of him who passionately loved you, and you will divine that, over a book which was yours, he could only think of love. In that word, beautiful in all languages, but most so in yours – *Amor mio* – is comprised my existence here and hereafter . . . my destiny rests with you, and you are a woman, seventeen years of age [sic] and two out of a convent. I wish that you had stayed there, with all my heart – or at least, that I had never met you in your married state.

'But all this is too late. I love you, and you love me – at least, you *say* so, and *act* as if you *did* so, which last is a great consolation in all events. But *I* more than love you, and cannot cease to love you.'

Almost incredibly, in August, the Count offered Byron the vacant ground floor of his palace. Byron moved in, and sent to Venice for Allegra. The Count's motives are mysterious: Teresa later said that she thought her husband had enjoyed basking in the company of such a distinguished figure, and that, anyway, 'the Count was a man different from others – eccentric – seeing things from a point of view peculiar to himself and very often even indulgent and almost generous.'

Another motive was perhaps revealed in the almost immediate request to Byron for the loan of quite a large sum of money. When Byron refused, the Count flew into a temper, and turned on Teresa, who immediately fell ill and insisted on returning to Venice. Byron accompanied her; they went first to his Palazzo, and then to La Mira. There he worked on *Don Juan* and on his memoirs, which, in a white leather bag, he handed to Tom Moore when the latter visited him. 'It contains', he said, 'a detailed account of my marriage and its consequence.' Moore felt he was carrying a sack of gunpowder.

Byron wrote, a little later, to Lady Byron, telling her that he had written the memoirs, and that they were perfectly open to her inspection – indeed, he would promise to omit anything she felt to be false. 'You will perhaps say *why* write my life?' he told her. 'Alas! I say so too – but they who have traduced it – and blasted

The Memoirs

82

Bologna, by Richard Bonington

it – and branded me -- should know – that it is they – and not I – are the cause – It is no great pleasure to have lived – and less to live over again the details of existence – but the last becomes sometimes a necessity and even a duty.'

In October, Count Guiccioli arrived in Venice. For a month he had done nothing; but Teresa's father had at last convinced him that a public scandal must be rebuked. While Byron lay in bed with a fever, the Count and his wife argued violently downstairs. In the end, she was persuaded to return with her husband to Ravenna.

Byron had promised the Count not to come to Ravenna, and seriously thought of going home to England. But one thing and another – Allegra was ill, and then the hard winter of 1819–20 discouraged travel – delayed him; so he went on with Canto II of *Don Juan*. Perhaps his separation from Teresa contributed to the lovely stanzas telling of the idyllic affair between Juan and the beautiful Haidée:

They were alone, but not alone as they
*   Who shut in chambers think it loneliness;*
The silent ocean, and the starlight bay,
*   The twilight glow, which momently grew less,*
The voiceless sands, and dropping caves, that lay
*   Around them, made them to each other press,*
As if there were no life beneath the sky
Save theirs, and that their life could never die.

They fear'd no eyes nor ears on that lone beach,
*   They felt no terrors from the night; they were*
All in all to each other; though their speech
*   Was broken words, they thought a language there, –*
And all the burning tongues the passions teach
*   Found in one sigh the best interpreter*
Of nature's oracle – first love – that all
Which Eve has left her daughters since her fall.

And there is indeed a sense in which Byron's last love was also his first; certainly it was his most intense. At Christmas he could no longer stay away from Teresa, and on Christmas Eve, despite his promise, he arrived at Ravenna. Everyone seemed delighted to see him.

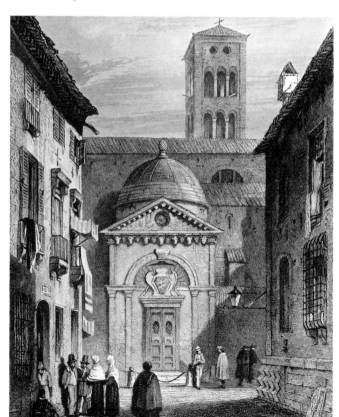

Dante's tomb at Ravenna

Count Pietro Gamba,
Teresa's younger brother.
'He shows character and talent –
Big eyebrows! and a stature which
he has enriched, I think. . . . His head
is a little too hot for revolutions –
he must not be too rash.'

By now, the first canto of *Juan* had appeared in England; and Annabella, with a sense of humour one might have thought lacking in her, rather appreciated it. On New Year's Eve, Byron wrote her a melancholy letter, asking for a remembrance of their daughter:

'This time five years . . . I was on my way to our funeral marriage. . . . That I think of you is but too obvious. . . .'

Count Guiccioli, who had been inclined to pick petty quarrels with Byron, suddenly offered him again a part of the Palazzo. 'Certainly the offer might appear strange', wrote Teresa in her own memoirs; 'but people were accustomed to consider the Count *an eccentric*, and after a few days they stopped talking about it.' Byron moved into an upper floor; the cold weather broke; his humour improved, and he seemed to have given up all thoughts of returning to England, where *Don Juan* had caused a mild sensation – Lady Caroline Lamb appeared at a masquerade as the Don!

Yet despite (or perhaps because of) his quiet life, he was beginning to grow restless, and perhaps almost welcomed the Count's sudden announcement, in May, that his attentions to Teresa were no longer supportable. Teresa wanted to leave her husband immediately; but Byron urged caution. Count Gamba, her father, had always rather liked Byron, and applied to the Pope for a separation for his daughter – who had complained that Count Guiccioli had been harsh with her! May and June of 1820, combining dull provincial life with a domestic turmoil, cannot have been altogether comfortable months for Byron.

'Marino Faliero'   He was working now on *Marino Faliero*, an historical tragedy which he had started some months earlier. Becoming more and more interested in Italy's political troubles, he was accepted into some of the secret societies in which Count Gamba and his son Pietro were active, and which were planning insurrection in support of a revolution against the Bourbon rulers in Naples.

On 6 July 1820 the Pope granted Teresa her separation. She left her husband, and returned to her father's family at the Villa Gamba, a pleasant, cool house by the Montone River. Byron still lived at the Palazzo Guiccioli, but regularly rode out to the Villa Gamba (sometimes followed by spies engaged by Count Guiccioli, with whom on at least one occasion he came to blows). The Gambas were interested in astronomy, as well as politics, and Byron would sit quietly with them in the garden at twilight, watching the stars come up in the clear Italian air.

The Carbonari   During August, the Carbonari (the most famous of Italian secret societies, formed in the Kingdom of Naples during the French occupation with the aim of introducing a republican government) busily planned an uprising in Ravenna, to take place early in September. But all the secret societies were riddled with spies and counter-spies, and suddenly arrests were made. Though the Gambas, and Byron also, were suspected, they were unmolested. An order was issued to the local police to disarm Byron's servants; but it seems that they were too timid to execute it.

An atmosphere of melodrama (highly enjoyable to Byron) thickened: in December the commandant of the local troops was shot to death on Byron's doorstep. In January of 1821 the poet wrote to the Neapolitan rebels offering them 1,000 louis and his own services as a volunteer; the courier, when he was suddenly arrested, swallowed the letter to preserve it from the police.

A meeting of the Carbonari. 'My lower apartments are full of [Carbonari] bayonets, fusils, cartridges and what not. I suppose that they consider me a depot, to be sacrificed, in case of accidents.'

The Villa Gamba, Filetto

Naples, 1820: the Constitutional troops enter the City

'The Death of Sardanapalus', by Eugène Delacroix

Byron worked on. Canto V of *Don Juan* had been completed in December, and
was on its way to England. Now he started a new work – *Sardanapalus*, a tragedy
about a luxurious monarch fighting revolution. Again, as in everything he wrote,
there were elements of self-portraiture:

> *He must be roused. In his effeminate heart*
> *There is a careless courage which Corruption*
> *Has not all quenched, and latent energies,*
> *Repressed by circumstance, but not destroyed –*
> *Steeped, but not drowned, in deep voluptuousness.*

But while he worked on *Sardanapalus*, he still had great plans for *Don Juan*. He told Murray he wanted to set episodes in Italy, England and Germany – 'but I had not quite fixed whether to make him end in Hell, or in an unhappy marriage, not knowing which would be the severest.'

The proper care of Allegra (who was now four) was causing Byron some concern. Fearing that she might suffer during the physical violence of any possible revolution, he placed her in the convent of Bagnacavallo. Claire Clairmont violently opposed this (which was in itself enough to commend the plan to Byron); and so did Richard Hoppner and his wife (the British Consul in Venice who had helped care for the child over the past four years). But Teresa's family was delighted, and Byron told Hoppner: 'You know . . . that to allow the child to be with her mother . . . would be like absolute insanity if not worse; that even her health would not be attended to properly and to say nothing of the indecorum. . . . It is, besides, my wish that she should be a Roman Catholic, which I look upon as the best religion, as it is assuredly the oldest of the various branches of Christianity.'

In May, news reached Ravenna of the outbreak of the Greek war for independence – but Byron was too preoccupied with the failure of the proposed Italian uprisings to be much interested. Besides, he had started a new tragedy, *The Two Foscari*, 'The Two Foscari' based on the historical account of a Doge of Venice and his rebel son, both of whom died for love of the city. In July, just as he finished the play, the news came that Teresa's father and her brother Pietro had been arrested and exiled from the state of Romagna for their political activities. It seems that the authorities may have believed this a safe way of getting rid of Byron, the undesirable alien whose name lent weight to revolutionary ideals. The Gambas found refuge in Florence; although Teresa was heartbroken at leaving him, Byron remained in Ravenna and started work on another tragedy, *Cain*, in which he examined the Biblical 'Cain' story which had fascinated him since his childhood. It was to arouse, when it was published, more outraged protests than any other of his works, although Sir Walter Scott – accepting the Dedication – declared that in it Byron had 'certainly matched Milton on his own ground'. Goethe said that *Cain*'s beauty was 'such as we shall not see a second time in the world', and Shelley called it 'apocalyptic; a revelation never before communicated to man'.

Cain could scarcely have commended itself to the general reader in an age that was dominated (despite its excesses) by the Evangelical revolution in religion. The followers of Whitefield and Wesley were unlikely to be happy with Cain's outburst against the inevitability of man's earthly lot:

> *For what should I be gentle? for a war*
> *With all the elements ere they will yield*
> *The bread we eat? For what must I be grateful?*

For being dust, and grovelling in the dust,
Till I return to dust? If I am nothing –
For nothing shall I be an hypocrite,
And seem well-pleased with pain?

or its admiring references to

Souls who dare look the Olympian tyrant in
His everlasting face, and tell him that
His evil is not good.

The Examiner indeed reported that George IV himself 'expressed his disapprobation of the blasphemy and licentiousness of Lord Byron's writings', though Byron said he was not prepared to listen to the voices of outraged piety. 'As to myself,' he wrote, 'I shall not be deterred by any outcry; your present public hate me, but they shall not interrupt the march of my mind, nor prevent me from telling those who are attempting to trample on all thought, that their thrones shall yet be rocked to their foundations.'

'Cain and Abel', engraved by J. Smith

Pisa from the Campo Santo

In August, Shelley arrived on a visit, and Byron – who had been months without being able to talk with an intelligent fellow-countryman – sat up until 5 a.m. next morning with him. He read Shelley the most recent cantos of *Don Juan*, and his friend wrote to the novelist Thomas Love Peacock (who in his *Nightmare Abbey* was to satirize the gloomier aspects of Byron's philosophy): 'I think every word of it is pregnant with immortality.' In the same letter he drew an amusing sketch of Byron's domestic life:

'Lord B.'s establishment consists besides servants, of ten horses, eight enormous dogs, three monkeys, five cats, an eagle, a crow and a falcon; and all these, except the horses, walk about the house, which every now and then resounds with their unarbitrated quarrels, as if they were the masters of it.' And he re-opened the letter to add: 'I find that my enumeration of the animals in this Circean Palace was defective, and that in a material point. I have just met on the grand staircase five peacocks, two guinea hens, and an Egyptian crane.'

Byron agreed to move from Ravenna to Pisa, where he could be near the Shelleys and Teresa. Shelley managed to find for him a large old sixteenth-century palace on the Lungarno; it was quiet, and had a little enclosed garden. The Gambas moved to Pisa in preparation, they hoped, for Byron's arrival there; and Shelley wrote to England to ask his friend Leigh Hunt to come to join him and Byron in the foundation of a new literary magazine.

Robert Southey. 'That poor, insane creature, the Laureate.'

Leigh Hunt had been editor of both *The Examiner* and *The Reflector*, and in 1813 had gone to prison for libelling the Prince Regent in the former periodical. Byron had visited him while he was in gaol, and was generally sympathetic to his radical aims; in 1818 there had been some talk of Hunt coming to Italy. Now Shelley wrote to him:

'He [Byron] proposes that you should come out and go shares with him and me in a periodical work, to be conducted here; in which each of the contracting parties should publish all their original compositions, and share the profits.'

It is difficult to say precisely how enthusiastic Byron was about this proposal; but at all events he allowed Shelley to put it forward while he began the tedious business of packing for his move to Pisa, and while he was doing so threw off in *'A Vision of* a few days a long new poem – *A Vision of Judgement*. He had been reading a poem *Judgement'* of the same title by Robert Southey, the Poet Laureate: an extraordinarily fulsome work in which the poet in a trance saw George III rise from the tomb and apply for admission to Paradise, aided by a testimonial from Wellington. In a Preface, Southey had attacked Byron, the author of 'monstrous combinations of horrors and mockery, lewdness and impiety'.

92

In 106 stanzas, Byron laid about him in reply. It is an extremely enjoyable poem, in which George III comes off badly, but the Laureate comes off even worse. There are, incidentally, some noble stanzas – this one, for instance, describing the meeting of Satan and St Michael:

> He and the sombre, silent Spirit met –
>   They knew each other both for good and ill;
> Such was their power, that neither could forget
>   His former friend and future foe; but still
> There was a high, immortal, proud regret
>   In either's eye, as if 'twere less their will
> Than destiny to make the eternal years
> Their date of war, and their 'champ clos' the spheres.

On the morning of 29 October 1821 Byron departed from Ravenna, leaving his banker Pellegrino Ghigi to look after 'a Goat with a broken leg, an ugly peasant Dog, a Bird of the heron type which would eat only fish, a Badger on a chain, and two ugly old monkeys'. And, of course, Allegra, still in the convent at Bagnacavallo.

Near Empoli, thirty miles from Florence, Byron was scribbling at a lyric poem as the public coach from Pisa passed his carriage. Inside it, unnoticed, sat Claire Clairmont, on her way back to Florence.

On 2 November Byron arrived at Pisa. He was delighted with the Casa *Pisa* Lanfranchi, the enclosed garden, and the mildness of the weather. He fell into a

Villa Lanfranchi, Pisa. 'I have got here into a famous old feudal palazzo, on the Arno, large enough for a garrison, with dungeons below and cells in the walls, and so full of Ghosts that the learned Fletcher (my valet) has begged leave to change his room.'

Jane and Edward Williams

new routine: visiting Teresa daily, and becoming the centre of a small group of admirers – notably, of course, Shelley and Mary Shelley. He was introduced to Edward and Jane Williams – a lieutenant living with a fellow officer's wife, with whom he had eloped. Williams was delighted with Byron: 'He is all sunshine, and good humour with which the elegance of his language and the brilliancy of his wit cannot fail to inspire those who are near him.' Thomas Medwin, another friend of the Shelleys, was also introduced, and became a regular guest at the weekly dinner-parties Byron began to give for his men friends. Medwin took some careful notes of Byron's table-talk, which he thought was splendid:

'His ideas flow without effort, without his having occasion to think. As to his letters, he is not nice about expressions or words – there are no concealments in him. . . . He hates argument, and never argues for victory. He gives everyone an opportunity of sharing in the conversation, and has the art of turning it to subjects that may bring out the person with whom he converses.'

94

Byron at Pisa, 1822. 'He is now quite reformed, and is leading a most sober and decent life as *cavaliere servente* to a very pretty Italian woman.' – Shelley

Byron's thoughts seemed to turn constantly towards England, and to Annabella and his daughter Ada. Lady Byron had sent him a lock of Ada's hair, and writing to thank her, he said: 'I . . . thank you for the inscription of the date and name, and I will tell you why – I believe that they are the only two or three words of your handwriting in my possession. For your letters I returned; and except the two words, or rather the one word "Household", written twice in an old account book, I have no other.' But he never posted the letter.

Edward John Trelawny.
'If he will learn to tell the
truth and wash his hands we
may make a gentleman of
him yet.'

Trelawny   In the new year, the company of Byron's friends was enlarged by the larger-than-life figure of that extraordinary Cornish adventurer Edward John Trelawny. He had already had some remarkable piratical adventures in his life (though perhaps not so remarkable as he indicated in retelling them), and he said he had come to Italy expressly to meet Shelley and Byron. In his *Last Days of Shelley and Byron* he leaves the most vivid description of their lives in Pisa. Although he is scarcely to be taken literally, his book is an evocative and pithy one.

Byron thought him the personification of his own Corsair, and was soon persuaded to join Shelley in having two boats built, in which they could all sail in the Bay of Spezia. He could now afford such luxuries, for Lady Byron's mother, Lady Noel, had died in January, and Byron's income was doubled as a result. (One condition of the will was that he should adopt the Noel arms, and he began signing himself 'Noel Byron'.) Moreover, Murray had sent him 2,500 guineas for the three new cantos of *Don Juan*, and the three plays *Sardanapalus*, *The Two Foscari* and *Cain*. They had all been published in December 1821, and already a clergyman in Pisa had preached against *Cain*.

96

It was at this time that Byron's relationship with Shelley began to sour a little. Shelley felt (and undoubtedly with some cause) that Byron was less than enthusiastic about helping Hunt, who was unable to pay the fares for himself and his family to Italy. Then Claire was in great anxiety about Allegra, who, she suspected, was not properly cared for at the convent. But Byron refused to listen to Shelley's mediation in the matter. He was also short-tempered because, in an attempt to lose weight, he was living almost entirely on a diet of biscuits and soda-water (from which, Trelawny says, 'to allay all the eternal hunger gnawing at his vitals' he would occasionally depart, making up 'a horrid mess of cold potatoes, rice, fish, or greens, deluged in vinegar' which he would 'gobble like a famished dog').

In March there was a farcical yet serious incident outside the walls of Pisa. One day when Byron was out riding with his friends, the party came into conflict with a sergeant-major of the Tuscan Royal Light Horse; he jostled the party and, when remonstrated with, knocked Shelley senseless from his horse. Byron's coachman, in an excess of zeal, attacked the sergeant-major, seriously wounding him; and there was a considerable public outcry against 'the Englishmen'. Though the soldier recovered and the matter died down, the authorities remained extremely suspicious of Byron and his movements while he remained in Italy.

The Casa Magni, San Terenzo: Shelley's house

Death of Allegra   In the next month came a more serious and personal blow; a letter from Ghigi, Byron's banker in Ravenna, brought news that Allegra was suffering from fever. On 20 April she was 'stricken with a convulsive catarrhal attack, and a little after ten she expired'.

It is difficult to gauge Byron's feelings about Allegra's death. He may have had one or two pangs of conscience, for although he wrote to Shelley: 'I do not know that I have anything to reproach in my conduct, and certainly nothing in my feelings and intentions towards the dead', he went on: 'But it is a moment when we are apt to think that, if this or that had been done, such event might have been prevented.' The truth seems to be that while Allegra was in the convent, Byron was affectionately disposed; but he certainly was impatient of her presence in his household.

He had the body embalmed and sent to England to be buried in Harrow church, asking that a tablet should be put up to her memory, bearing the inscription: 'In memory of Allegra, daughter of G.G. Lord Byron, who died at Bagnacavallo, in Italy, April 20th 1822, aged five years and three months.' But so infamous was his name in England, that the Rector refused to put up any tablet bearing it; the churchwardens even refused the little body burial in the church. Its precise burial-place is unknown, although it is believed to lie beneath the flagstones of the south porch. There is still no commemorative stone.

At the end of May, Byron settled into the Villa Dupuy at Montenero, and awaited the arrival of his now completed boat. He had decided to call it the *Bolivar* – after the South American patriot and revolutionary. Shelley's boat arrived at the same time, and Byron decided that it should be called the *Don Juan*; he had the name painted largely on the sail. Shelley was not pleased; he had wanted to call his boat the *Ariel* – but when he had Byron's inscription clumsily removed from the sail, the latter flew into a rage. However, the boat was always known as the *Ariel*, and the two poets remained on speaking terms. In an access of pride and showmanship, Byron had two cannon made, with his coronet mounted on them, and placed them on the *Bolivar's* deck. The local authorities promptly set up so many regulations about when and where the boat might be permitted to sail, that Byron scarcely set foot on her.

Leigh Hunt   At the beginning of July, his irritation mounted with the arrival of Leigh Hunt, who was installed at the Villa Lanfranchi with his wife – a snobbish woman who hated Italy and the Italians – and a number of children. It was doubly inconvenient for Byron to have the Hunts at the villa, for now the Tuscan government, in its turn, had exiled the Gamba family, and Byron felt that he should support them in their exile. But how could he leave Pisa, with the Hunts and their Yahoo children overrunning his house? Mrs Hunt and Fletcher spent the days grumbling about the Italian servants, and Byron was driven to distraction by the children.

98

(He had never liked children, anyway; years before, he had told Augusta: 'I abominate them so much that I have always had the greatest respect for the character of Herod.')

However, the Gambas were given temporary asylum at Lucca, and Teresa was allowed to stay with Byron in Pisa; so for a while a somewhat uneasy peace descended. Hunt remembered how the days ran:

'Our manner of life was this. Lord Byron, who used to sit up at night, writing *Don Juan* (which he did under the influence of gin and water), rose late in the morning. He breakfasted; read; lounged about, singing an air, generally out of Rossini, and in a swaggering style, though in a voice at once small and veiled; then took a bath, and was dressed; and coming downstairs, was heard, still singing, in the court-yard, out of which the garden ascended at the back of the house. The servants at the same time brought out two or three chairs. . . . We then lounged about, or sat and talked, Madame Guiccioli with her sleek tresses descending after her toilet to join us. . . . When the heat of the day declined, we rode out, either on horse-back or in a barouche, generally towards the forest. He was a good rider, and kept a firm seat. . . .'

The *Don Juan* and the *Bolivar*. 'People think I must be a bit of a sailor from my writings. All the sea-terms I use are from authority, and they cost me time, toil and trouble to look them out; but you will find me a land-lubber. I hardly know the stem from the stern.'

'Lerici – The Castle' ▶
by Richard Bonington

Mary Shelley:
'What changes! What a life!
We now appear tranquil; yet
who knows what wind – but
I will not prognosticate evil;
we have had enough of it.'

The temporary peace was broken on 11 July, when a distracted Trelawny arrived to announce that Shelley and Williams, who had set out four days before to sail from Leghorn to Lerici, were missing. The watchers on the shore had seen a sudden storm arise, which obscured their sight of the *Ariel*. When the storm cleared, there was no sign of the vessel.

Death of Shelley Mary Shelley and Jane Williams called at Pisa, then went on to Leghorn, where Trelawny was by now making inquiries. Gradually the evidence accumulated. A wrecked boat came ashore; then, on the sixteenth, two bodies were washed on to the beach near Viareggio, and two days later, another. Trelawny identified the last as Shelley, a copy of Keats's poems open in his pocket. Byron, perhaps a little ashamed of his recent coolness to Shelley (who was still his closest literary friend), wrote to Murray: 'He was, without exception, the *best* and least selfish man I ever knew. I never knew one who was not a beast in comparison.'

Trelawny persuaded the authorities to allow him to cremate the bodies of Shelley and Williams on the beach, and take the ashes to Rome for burial. On 15 July Byron and he witnessed the burning of the bodies; incense and wine were thrown on the flames, and as Shelley's body burned, Byron swam out to the *Bolivar*, anchored off shore, and was badly sunburned; in the evening, in hysterical reaction, they both got drunk.

By now Byron had three new cantos of *Don Juan* ready; Hunt was pressing on with arrangements for the new journal, which at first was to have been called the *Hesperides*, but eventually came out as *The Liberal*. Byron contributed *The Vision of Judgement* to the first issue, which appeared on 15 October 1822. It was not well received – many of Byron's friends advised him against a continued association with it – and although he contributed to the next three issues, he played a decreasingly important part in running the magazine. His contribution to the first issue may have helped to sell it, but did not in the end help its publisher, Leigh Hunt's brother John. In 1824, John Hunt was prosecuted for 'calumniating the late king, and wounding the feelings of his present Majesty', thus endangering the public peace. Three days after Byron's burial, Hunt was fined £100 for the offence.

Within a few weeks of the publication of the first issue of *The Liberal*, Murray had received the manuscript of the three new cantos of *Don Juan*. He was horrified. 'I declare to you', he wrote, 'they were so outrageously shocking that I would not publish them if you were to give me your Estate – Title and Genius – for Heaven's sake revise them. . . .'

These cantos do not seem, now, any more rash or any more sensual than the rest of the poem; but Murray had an ear to the ground, and the upsurge of indignation against the author of *The Vision of Judgement* suggested that the time was not convenient for the new cantos to be offered as ammunition to Byron's enemies. But the poet himself was, of course, furious, and threatened to withdraw his work from Murray. He wrote steadily on, finishing Canto XII by 9 December, and Cantos XIII, XIV and XV by the end of March 1823.

In the autumn of 1822, he had moved from Pisa into the Casa Saluzzo in Genoa, arranging for the Hunts to share a house about a mile away with Mary Shelley. Though he was relieved to be rid of their immediate presence, he was not well; another period of fasting had weakened him, and his general health was not good. Somehow, too, his relationship with Teresa was not as blandly happy as it had been. Perhaps the routine of a highly domestic affair was beginning to bore him. In any case, he was delighted when a party of English people arrived in Genoa, led by the beautiful and witty Lady Blessington, her husband, her sister, and their young friend the Count d'Orsay. The Countess was a leader of London society, whose immensely rich husband made it possible for her to entertain freely and to travel widely.

The Albaro Hill, Genoa, where the Casa Saluzzo stood

Leigh Hunt. 'He is a good man, with some poetical elements in his chaos.'

Count d'Orsay

Byron welcomed the opportunity to discuss England, poetry, society, with Lady Blessington and the elegant Count d'Orsay. She, after at first being disconcerted by his old-fashioned clothes and what she took to be an untoward flippancy in his conversation, grew to like and admire him. She wrote in her diary:

'His hair has already much of silver among its dark brown curls; its texture is very silky, and although it retreats from his temples, leaving his forehead very bare, its growth at the sides and back of his head is abundant. . . . His voice and accent are particularly clear and harmonious, but somewhat effeminate; and his enunciation is so distinct that, though his general tone in speaking is low, not a word is lost. His laugh is musical, but he rarely indulged in it during our [first] interview.' Despite herself, Lady Blessington was a little shocked by the freedom of Byron's conversation, by 'the perfect *abandon* with which he converses to recent acquaintances, on subjects which even friends would think too delicate for discussion.'

In London at about this time, a London Greek Committee had been formed to help the cause of Greek independence. Greece still had an enormous sentimental appeal to the cultivated Englishman – an appeal epitomized in the Elgin Marbles, which seemed to represent to insular Englishmen the whole spirit of culture and nobility. Knowing nothing, or little, of the muddled state of Greek politics (and indeed, of the war), radical Englishmen were more enthusiastic for the Greek cause than for any other of their own time – poets like Campbell and Byron had denounced the seizure of the Danish fleet as an act of unwonted aggression, and the dethronement of Napoleon as petty and spiteful.

Rumours of Byron's interest in Greece had reached the Committee – and, of course, there had been the evidence of the lyric included in Canto III of *Juan*:

The Elgin Marbles in London   *Such dim-conceived glories of the brain*
Bring round the heart an undescribable feud;
So do these wonders a most dizzy pain . . . – Keats

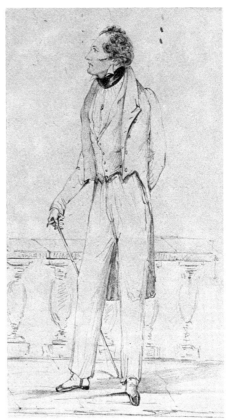

Lady Blessington. (*right*) Byron at Genoa, sketched by Count d'Orsay

> *The mountains look on Marathon –*
> *And Marathon looks on the sea;*
> *And musing there an hour alone,*
> *I dream'd that Greece might still be free....*

So a Committee member, Edward Blaquiere, was instructed to call on Byron with a Greek delegate, Andreas Luriottis, and try to enlist his active help.

The time was opportune. Lady Blessington and her party would eventually leave Genoa, and Byron could not face the prospect of a continuation of what had become an ineffably dull routine. He discussed the situation eagerly with Blaquiere and Luriottis; in April was elected a member of the London Greek Committee; and by May was writing to tell them that his 'first wish' was to go to Greece in person. 'I do not want to limit my own contribution', he told the secretary, 'but more especially if I can get to Greece myself, I should devote whatever resources I can muster of my own, to advancing the great object.'

And so Byron prepared to reach the climax of that radicalism which had been a conscious and unconscious motif of his life since his early youth. Painfully proud of his rank as an English nobleman, from the very moment when the name 'Byron Dominus' sent him crying from the classroom of Aberdeen Grammar School, he was also very conscious of the depths of moral insufficiency which crippled the peerage – a peerage still enormously strong and influential at the close of the Napoleonic wars.

His strong Calvinist streak allied him, in a sense, with such men as John Newton, Joseph and Isaac Milner, John Bowdler – with the Methodist and Evangelical movements. Yet he agreed with Scott, when the latter suggested that Byron's conversion to Catholicism would not be surprising: and indeed *Childe Harold*, *Prometheus*, *Manfred*, *Cain*, *Sardanapalus*, all have the sense of sin as a central point. Byron felt the constant presence of sin and evil as Shelley, for instance, never did; his concern for the under-dog – for instance, the Nottingham stocking weavers – naturally followed.

His radical instincts grew stronger as his intelligence developed; he saw Waterloo, for instance, as a triumph for reaction. 'Napoleon! – this week will decide his fate. All seems against him; but I believe and hope he will win. . . . What right have we to prescribe sovereigns to France? Oh for a Republic!' Gradually, the consciousness of the changes which were to come in Europe in the century after his death became important to him. The French Revolution was now a part of the history of his life; he felt that 'the king-times are fast finishing. There will be blood shed like water, and tears like mist; but the peoples will conquer in the end. I shall not live to see it, but I foresee it.'

His meetings with the Carbonari were not mere adventuring. He was in complete intellectual sympathy with the movement, and if there had been a rising in Ravenna in 1821, he would have been in the thick of it. He became, more and more, a republican – and with the silly and corrupt English court at home, small wonder. 'There is nothing left for Mankind but a Republic', he wrote in his journal in 1821; 'and I think that there are hopes of such. The two Americas (South and North) have it; Spain and Portugal approach it; all thirst for it. Oh Washington!' His admiration for Simón Bolívar, who liberated Colombia and Venezuela from Spanish rule, was so great that he seriously considered emigrating to South America in 1822.

But now, Greece! His admiration and love for the country had never wavered since his first visit, and while his attention had been focused elsewhere, he only needed the presence of Blaquiere and Luriottis to turn it again to the war of independence. This time his eye was steady and his determination unshakeable:

Simon Bolivar

Louis XVIII at the Tuileries, March 1815

The dead have been awakened – shall I sleep?
The World's at war with tyrants – shall I crouch?
The harvest's ripe – and shall I pause to reap?
I slumber not; the thorn is in my Couch;
Each day a trumpet soundeth in mine ear,
Its echo in my heart –

Ten months later, he was to lie dead at Missolonghi, and the whole of Greece in mourning.

For the moment, however, there was the embarrassment of breaking the news to Teresa. Writing to his friend Douglas Kinnaird (who was making arrangements in London to cover the costs of the expedition), he grumbled:

'I am doing all I can to get away, but I have all kinds of obstacles thrown in my way by the "absurd woman-kind", who seems determined on sacrificing herself in every way, and preventing me from doing any good, and all without reason. . . . If she makes a scene (and she has a turn that way) we shall have another romance, and tale of ill-usage, and abandonment, and Lady Carolining, and Lady Byroning . . . all cut and dry. There never was a man who gave up so much to women, and all I have gained by it has been the character of treating them harshly.'

Unable to muster the courage to break the news himself, Byron persuaded her brother Pietro to tell Teresa; for Pietro was to accompany him. Her first reaction

Byron
Arm! Arm! it is – it is –
the cannon's opening roar!

was that, of course, she would go too; and it took considerable tact to dissuade her. Byron turned his attention to the arrangements for the voyage: raising money in London, he also sold the *Bolivar* to Lord Blessington for 400 guineas (carefully removing the two cannon, which might be useful), and bought from Lady Blessington her Arabian horse Mameluke to carry him into battle. He designed grand uniforms for himself and his servants, and magnificent helmets bearing his motto, *Crede Byron*, and coat of arms for himself, Pietro and Trelawny.

In mid-June, all was ready. He parted with Teresa and went on board the *Hercules*, which sailed from Genoa on 16 July with Trelawny, Pietro Gamba, a young Doctor Bruno, five servants (including the ubiquitous Fletcher, and a huge and ugly gondolier, Tita Falcieri), five horses, Byron's bulldog Moretto, and a large Newfoundland, Lyon. At Leghorn the company was joined by a Scot, James Hamilton Browne – who brought with him, incidentally, a message of goodwill from Goethe, expressed in adulatory verse. As the *Hercules* sailed on down the coast, Byron passed the time by boxing with Trelawny or fencing with Pietro Gamba; shooting at empty bottles or live geese; and swimming every day.

The *Hercules* had been making for Zante; but Browne, who had served in the Ionian Islands (and had been dismissed because of his Hellenic sympathies), recommended changing course for Cephalonia, which was governed by Colonel   *Cephalonia* Charles James Napier, the only English Resident who was openly in favour of the Greek cause. So, on 2 August 1823, anchor was dropped near Argostoli.

Argostoli, Cephalonia

It soon became clear to Byron that the situation in Greece was extremely confused: the Greeks were divided into several factions, each jealous of the other, and until he was more sure of the situation it was obviously best to stay where he was. So the party lived for the time being on board the *Hercules*, went riding and swimming, and made friends with Colonel Napier.

It was in Cephalonia that Byron met Dr James Kennedy, a medical officer on the island, and an eager and convinced evangelist who conceived it his vocation to convert the poet. Kennedy's friends encouraged him, no doubt anticipating sport; but although Byron was never averse to baiting a Methodist, basically he took his discussions with Kennedy seriously – as may be seen from the latter's book *Conversations on Religion with Lord Byron*, which was published in 1830, and which incidentally gives perhaps the best impression extant of Byron's style of conversation.

'It is all a mystery. I feel most things, but I know nothing. . . .' Byron may have satirized religion, but his attitude to it was far from frivolous. He believed profoundly in the immortality of the soul, although 'how far our future life will be individual, or, rather, how far it will at all resemble our *present* existence, is another question.'

He was always quick to excuse himself to anyone who felt that his poetry was anti-religious. When Tom Moore complained of the irreligion of the characters of his drama *Werner* (1822), he replied: 'Can I never convince you that *I* have no such opinions as the characters in that drama, which seems to have frightened everyone? Yet *they* are nothing to the expressions in Goethe's *Faust* (which are ten times hardier), and not a whit more bold than those of Milton's Satan. My ideas of a character may run away with me. . . . I am no enemy to religion, but the contrary. . . . I think people can never have *enough* of religion, if they are to have any.'

Byron's religious discussions with Kennedy had little result, so far as his education in conventional religious practices was concerned: he still refused to be convinced by dogma –

> *Between two worlds Life hovers like a star,*
> *'Twixt Night and Morn, upon the horizon's verge.*
> *How little do we know that which we are!*
> *How less what we may be! The eternal surge*
> *Of Time and Tide rolls on and bears afar*
> *Our bubbles; as the old burst, new emerge,*
> *Lashed from the foam of ages; while the graves*
> *Of Empires heave but like some passing waves.*

Byron and Lyon.
'Lyon, you are no rogue, Lyon;
thou art an honest fellow; thou
art more faithful than man,
Lyon, I trust thee more . . . I
love thee, thou art
my faithful dog!'

Teresa Guiccioli, by Bartolini.
'Pray be as cheerful and tranquil as you
can. . . . You may be sure that the
moment I can join you again, will be
as welcome to me as at any period of
our recollection.' – October 1823

The delays forced upon him by the internal situation in Greece depressed him;
also he was not well – during a visit to Ithaca he fell ill and took some time to
recover. Meanwhile, the news of his arrival having spread through Greece, every
post brought new requests for his presence or his money, from the various quarrelling
factions. But he refused to be drawn into their dissensions: early in September he
left the *Hercules* and moved into a small villa on shore. 'I was a fool to come here',
he wrote to Teresa; and gave up writing his journal because he 'found I could
not help abusing the Greeks in it.'

Not that he ever seriously considered withdrawing his support: indeed, he lent
the Greeks £4,000 for the payment of their fleet, and publicly at least was a
consistent propagandist for their cause. Nevertheless three months passed before,
Missolonghi at the end of December 1823, he left Cephalonia for Missolonghi, at the invitation
of the great Greek patriot, Prince Mavrocordatos. With him he took Fletcher,
Dr Bruno, Tita Falcieri, and a new young Greek page, Loukas Chalandritsanos.

After an eventful voyage (the fast *mistico* in which he sailed was twice almost
taken by Turkish warships, and then nearly wrecked) he reached Missolonghi on
4 January, to be greeted enthusiastically by Prince Mavrocordatos and five thousand
soldiers – including six hundred Suliotes who were placed under his command
(and for whom he had to provide). He enjoyed himself immensely – and revealed
no small talent for military command and organization.

Vathi, Ithaca

Lord Byron attended by his Suliote Guards

He moved into a large house, with a yard near by where he could drill his mercenaries. Even the oppressiveness of the town – damp and marshy, with slummy houses and overcrowded living conditions – could not depress him now. He decided, in consultation with the Prince (an ambitious, and probably deceitful man), to concentrate on a plan for the siege and capture of Lepanto. To encourage the Greeks, he helped to start a newspaper – the *Hellenica Chronica*. It had few subscribers in Greece, but did some good in London as a propaganda agent.

Though his mercenaries quarrelled and fought, though the Greeks still argued among themselves, though the dampness of the atmosphere tended to give him the fever, Byron was happy: for the first time for a number of years, he felt he was involved in events larger than himself. Since his last sustained work on *Don Juan* months earlier, he had written practically no poetry; but on the eve of his birthday, tired and unwell, but conscious that he was in Greece and in arms for the cause of freedom, he began a new poem. On his birthday, he handed it to Colonel Leicester Stanhope, an agent of the London Greek Committee now stationed at Missolonghi. 'This', he said, 'I think is better than what I usually write.' The poem was almost an invocation to death:

> *'Tis time this heart should be unmoved,*
> *Since others it hath ceased to move:*
> *Yet, though I cannot be beloved,*
> *Still let me love!*

My days are in the yellow leaf;
   The flowers and fruits of Love are gone;
The worm, the canker, and the grief
         Are mine alone!

The fire that on my bosom preys
   Is lone as some Volcanic isle;
No torch is kindled at its blaze –
         A funeral pile.

The hope, the fear, the jealous care,
   The exalted portion of the pain
And power of love, I cannot share,
         But wear the chain.

But 'tis not thus – and 'tis not here –
   Such thoughts should shake my soul, nor now,
Where glory decks the hero's bier,
         Or binds his brow.

The sword, the banner, and the field,
   Glory and Greece, around me see!
The Spartan, borne upon his shield,
         Was not more free.

Awake! (not Greece – she is awake!)
   Awake my spirit! Think through whom
Thy life-blood tracks its parent lake,
         And then strike home!

Tread those reviving passions down,
   Unworthy manhood! – unto thee
Indifferent should the smile or frown
         Of Beauty be.

If thou regret'st thy youth, why live?
   The land of honourable death
Is here: – up to the Field, and give
         Away thy breath!

Seek out – less often sought than found –
   A soldier's grave, for thee the best;
Then look around, and choose thy ground,
         And take thy Rest.

Ada, a miniature of
Byron's daughter

This noble poem, written for his thirty-fifth birthday, was to be almost his last.

Mavrocordatos commissioned Byron to lead two thousand men to the relief of Lepanto – and it was soon plain that he expected the poet to bear the entire cost of the operation himself. Undismayed, Byron set about the necessary arrangements. He worked day and night, on the whole in high spirits but low health. The rain fell incessantly, and the house set in the marshes near the lagoon was unhealthy. But the approaching campaign fascinated him: Lepanto was the only Turkish fortress on the north shore of the Gulf of Corinth, and its capture would enable the Greeks to gain the Castle of Morea opposite, thus giving them command of the whole Gulf.

Illness   In the middle of February, overwork in dreadful conditions began to tell seriously on Byron. One day he collapsed in what appeared to be a kind of epileptic fit. Dr Bruno and Dr Millingen (a young English doctor sent out by the London Greek Committee) were sent for, and he was helped to bed. Dr Bruno immediately suggested that he should be bled; but Byron violently objected. However, eight leeches were applied to his temples – and when they were removed, the bleeding would not stop, so that he fainted from loss of blood. This was the first serious sign of the illness that was to kill him.

He recovered, however, and was soon again about his military preparations, which largely consisted of trying to keep his mercenaries, who rioted and fought continually among themselves, in some kind of order. His kindness to the Turkish

116

prisoners who were brought to Missolonghi caused comment, and did not commend him to some of his soldiers; but on the whole he was able to maintain a moderately disciplined atmosphere.

His health remained uncertain. Sometimes – as when a welcome letter from England brought him a miniature of Ada, of which he was enormously proud – he was in good spirits, and would express them in rather juvenile practical jokes (for instance, crowding a group of Suliotes into an upstairs room, and ordering them to jump up and down, simulating an earthquake to terrify a boring member of his entourage). But at other times, irritated and unwell, he would be morose and unpredictable; his household would have an almost surrealist atmosphere, with meals served at all hours, and the servants apparently interchanging their duties – except for the faithful Fletcher, the gondolier Tita, and the handsome and devoted Greek boy Loukas who, dressed in page's costume, was always at Byron's side.

Loukas Chalandritsanos

After his disastrous marriage and a long line of affairs – ranging from the passionate involvement with Lady Caroline through, he said himself, over two hundred minor affairs, to the final domestic liaison with Teresa – Byron's friendship with Loukas was his last romantic attachment. In April, moved perhaps by the boy's devotion to him (in what was, after all, potentially a dangerous situation), he wrote his last poem which, though Hobhouse claimed to have seen a note in Byron's hand stating that it was 'addressed to no one in particular', was obviously dedicated to the boy:

I watched thee on the breakers, when the rock
  Received our prow and all was storm and fear,
And bade thee cling to me through every shock;
  This arm would be thy bark, or breast thy bier.

I watched thee when the fever glazed thine eyes,
  Yielding my couch and stretched me on the ground
When overworn with watching, ne'er to rise
  From thence if thou an early grave hadst found.

The earthquake came, and rocked the quivering wall,
  And men and nature reeled as if with wine.
Whom did I seek around the tottering hall?
  For thee. Whose safety first provide for? Thine.

The spring weather was abominable: it rained every day, the roads were quagmires, and Byron was irritated by often having to miss his daily rides. He was continually unwell, the Greeks were pressing him for money (he received requests for over £11,250 in one day!), and new Greek intrigues undermined his nerves. He wrote to Murray on 25 February: 'My office here is no sinecure, so many parties and difficulties of every kind; but I will do what I can. Prince Mavrocordato is an excellent person, and does all in his power; but his situation is perplexing in the extreme. Still we have great hopes of the success of the contest. . . .'

Small wonder that Byron became, under these strains, short-tempered and irritable. Pietro Gamba later wrote:

'He was frequently angry about trifles – more so, indeed, than about matters of importance: but his anger was only momentary. Frequently he complained of not feeling himself well – of vertigoes in the head – of a disposition to faint – and occasionally he told me that he experienced a sort of alarm without any apparent cause.'

On 9 April 1824, he insisted on riding – despite Pietro's protests – in torrential rain, and overheated by exercise sat for some time in a boat which took him back to his house. Two hours later he fell ill; that evening he was in a fever and in pain. He slept well, and next day rode again; but the fever remained. Dr Millingen was

Byron and his doctors

with him in the evening, but did not consider him ill enough even to take his pulse. Later that night, Byron himself sent for Dr Bruno, complaining of severe pains. With the common practice of the time, Bruno gave him a strong purgative and recommended bleeding; but Byron refused.

As the fever persisted, so did the doctors' insistence that bleeding and continued purgatives would relieve it. Byron was unconvinced: 'Drawing blood from a nervous patient', he said with some percipience, 'is like loosening the chords of a

'Greece expiring on the Ruins of Missolonghi' by Delacroix

The isles of Greece, the isles of Greece!
  Where burning Sappho loved and sung,
Where grew the arts of war and peace,
  Where Delos rose, and Phoebus sprung!
Eternal summer gilds them yet,
But all, except their sun, is set.

musical instrument, the tones of which are already defective for want of sufficient tension. Before I became ill, you know yourself how weak and irritable I had become. Bleeding, by increasing this state, will inevitably kill me.'

But at last, as he grew weaker, his will-power was incapable of resisting the repeated insistence of the two doctors: he allowed himself to be bled. 'Come; you are, I see, a damned set of butchers', he said. 'Take away as much blood as you will, but have done with it.'

He was bled of three pounds of blood, and heavily dosed with purgatives. At last the doctors began to suspect that he might be seriously ill. Two more doctors were sent for, and arguments began among the four medical men as to the nature of the illness and the nature of its treatment. Three of them were opposed to the continued bleeding on which Dr Bruno insisted; but the latter, an opinionated and strong-minded young man, won – and on the morning of Easter Sunday, the dying man lost two more pounds of blood.

By now Byron himself knew his danger. He attempted to give Fletcher some instructions, some messages for his half-sister, his daughter, and for Lady Byron; but soon became delirious. His utter weakness placed him completely in the hands of his four doctors. While he was still conscious, they forced on him a concoction of 'senna, three ounces of Epsom salts, and three of castor oil'. Not unnaturally, he fell into a coma; and they immediately applied leeches, which bled him all night.

For twenty-four hours he remained unconscious. At about six o'clock on the evening of 19 April, Fletcher saw his eyelids flicker, and then be still. The doctors felt his pulse. Byron was dead. In his delirium, not long before, he had called out: 'The doctors have assassinated me!' Clearly, he was right.

The grief which his death brought was immediate: his servants all adored him, and the tears of Tita, of Loukas, of Pietro, even of the doctors, flowed freely. Prince Mavrocordatos immediately ordered the firing of minute guns; for twenty-four hours they boomed out over the town. The doctors set about the task of post-mortem (so hastily and with so little thoroughness that the precise cause of Byron's death can never be known), and of embalming the body to prepare it for its journey to England. Meanwhile, Fletcher was gathering up the dead man's clothes and scraps of paper with the poem to Loukas, the poem on his birthday, and the last few stanzas of *Don Juan*.

A case containing Byron's heart was buried with great ceremony at the church of San Spiridione in Missolonghi, after an official oration which was unofficially echoed in almost every town and village in Greece. The news of his death deprived the Greeks of a hero whose name was almost sacred to them – and whose reputation has survived, now, for almost one and a half centuries. Even when, at the low points of Anglo-Greek relations, the English names of some Greek streets have been changed, one name has been left undisturbed: almost every town has its *Odos Byronos*.

On 2 May the body left Missolonghi for home, with the mourning Fletcher and Byron's two dogs, Moretto and Lyon. Twelve days later, Hobhouse was awakened in London and handed a letter clumsily written by Fletcher:

'Sir – Forgive Me for this Intrusion which I now am under the Painfull Necessity of wrighting to you to Inform you of the Malloncolly News of My Lord Byron whom his no more he Departed This Miserable Life on the 19 of April after an Illness of onley 10 Days his Lordship Began by a Nervous Feavour and Terminated with an Inflammation on the Brains For want of being Bled in time which his Lordship Refused till it was Too Late. . . . Please to Excuse all Deffects for I scearseley Now what I either Say or Do for after 20 Years Services to My Lord he was more to me than a father and I am too much Distressed to now give a Correct accompt of every Pertickeler which I hope to Do at my arrival in England.'

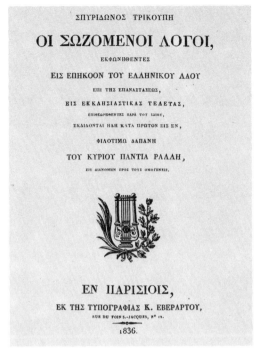

ΣΠΥΡΙΔΩΝΟΣ ΤΡΙΚΟΥΠΗ

OI ΣΩΖΟΜΕΝΟΙ ΛΟΓΟΙ,

ΕΚΦΩΝΗΘΕΝΤΕΣ

ΕΙΣ ΕΠΗΚΟΟΝ ΤΟΥ ΕΛΛΗΝΙΚΟΥ ΛΑΟΥ

ΕΠΙ ΤΗΣ ΕΠΑΝΑΣΤΑΣΕΩΣ,

ΕΙΣ ΕΚΚΛΗΣΙΑΣΤΙΚΑΣ ΤΕΛΕΤΑΣ,

ΕΠΙΘΕΩΡΗΘΕΝΤΕΣ ΠΑΡΑ ΤΟΥ ΙΔΙΟΥ,

ΕΚΔΙΔΟΝΤΑΙ ΗΔΗ ΚΑΤΑ ΠΡΩΤΟΝ ΕΙΣ ΕΝ,

ΦΙΛΟΤΙΜΩ ΔΑΠΑΝΗ

ΤΟΥ ΚΥΡΙΟΥ ΠΑΝΤΙΑ ΡΑΛΛΗ,

ΕΙΣ ΔΙΑΝΟΜΗΝ ΠΡΟΣ ΤΟΥΣ ΟΜΟΓΕΝΕΙΣ.

ΕΝ ΠΑΡΙΣΙΟΙΣ,

ΕΚ ΤΗΣ ΤΥΠΟΓΡΑΦΙΑΣ Κ. ΕΒΕΡΑΡΤΟΥ,
RUE DU FOIN S.-JACQUES, N° 13.
1836.

Title-page of Byron's funeral oration, delivered in
1824; published in Paris, 1836

John Murray

Hobhouse had the agonizing task of breaking the news to Augusta, while
Byron's heir (a cousin) told Lady Byron: 'She said she had no right to be considered by Lord Byron's friends, but she had her feelings.'

Hobhouse's mind turned next to the manuscript memoirs which Byron had
given to Tom Moore, and which were now in John Murray's hands. He
immediately contacted them both and told them that he was anxious to have the
manuscript destroyed immediately, for fear of the injury it might do to Byron's
reputation. Moore objected; but it was too late, for Hobhouse had persuaded
Augusta to agree to the burning of the manuscript. In an act of irreversible censor-
ship, Hobhouse (who had so often tried to induce Byron to tone down *Don Juan*)
and Murray ('the most timid of God's booksellers') destroyed Byron's own record
of his life, in Murray's rooms in Albemarle Street.

*Destruction of
the Memoirs*

The news of Byron's death spread through Europe: Carlyle felt as though he
'had lost a brother' and called Byron 'the noblest spirit in Europe'; Tennyson, a
boy of fourteen, felt that his world had crumbled, and scratched the words BYRON
IS DEAD into the sandstone near Somersby; Mary Shelley was shocked and

121

John Cam Hobhouse

regretted the coolness which had grown up between them after Shelley's death. Several ladies (including Lady Caroline Lamb and Lady Frances Webster) began appealing to Hobhouse for the discovery and return to them of their letters to Byron.

In Europe the effect of Byron's death was greater (and perhaps more lasting) than in England. Many French newspapers remarked that the two greatest men of the century, Napoleon and Byron, had disappeared at almost the same time. As a myth, his influence on the younger generation of Frenchmen was enormous; and Heine saw him as the most towering missionary of liberalism his generation had produced – the enemy of oppression and slavery, the nonconformist who would brook no interference with the freedom of the human spirit. Byron would scarcely have recognized himself in the inhuman heroic statue raised in the minds of many Europeans (any more than he would have recognized himself in the Antichrist many of his countrymen thought him).

On 5 July the body reached London. Since the Dean of Westminster refused permission for his burial in the Abbey, Hobhouse and Augusta had decided that he should lie in the family vault at Hucknall Torkard in Nottinghamshire. For two days the body lay in state, and crowds clamoured for admission: 'but very few persons of any name or note', Hobhouse sadly wrote in his diary.

On 12 July the body set out for Hucknall, through crowded streets. But Byron's fellow-peers showed a great reluctance to pay their respects. Their reasons were probably more political than social, although many of them had taken offence at his private life and his public writings. The British government was officially neutral in the Greek struggle, and it was obviously felt that there should be no demonstration which might be construed as support for the Greeks – especially as the members of the London Greek Committee, whose representative Byron had been, were more or less of the extreme left – mostly radical Whigs.

So, although there were forty-seven carriages to follow the hearse, many of them *The funeral* were empty: sent as a gesture of respect to a class, rather than a person, by those who disagreed with Byron's radicalism, or who even felt that he had, through his social actions and his private life, almost ceased to be an Englishman.

The procession moved up Oxford Street and Tottenham Court Road, up Highgate Hill, where Mary Shelley watched from a window, and on towards Nottingham. As the hearse passed Brocket Hall, Lady Caroline Lamb, its mistress, recovering from an illness, rode out with her husband. She asked whose funeral it was. Her husband made no reply.

Brocket Hall

Crowds watched the cortège pass through every town and village; at Nottingham the Town Clerk presented a resolution from the Corporation in tribute to Byron's memory, and would-be poets travelled to rest their hands for a moment on the coffin. On 16 July the small church at Hucknall was crowded for the funeral.

The confusion which almost immediately began between Byron the poet and Byron the romantic legend, has obscured his reputation ever since. While everyone remembers the legend, it is only comparatively recently that the poet has been allowed much virtue; and his masterpiece, *Don Juan*, is even now comparatively unread – less familiar, at any rate, than any work of comparable importance.

Yet Byron is an important poet, for reasons which have little to do with the sudden notoriety which *Childe Harold* brought to him in 1812, when new styles in collars and neckties were given his name, and when he wrote quickly and sometimes carelessly, knowing that everything he did write would be read with interest – if even for the wrong reasons.

His gift was not for the kind of poetry which the average reader could readily recognize as 'poetic'; when he did attempt to write the average, pathetic lyric which was popular in his time, the result was laughable:

> *When Friendship or Love our sympathies move,*
> *When Truth in a glance should appear,*
> *The lips may beguile with a dimple or smile,*
> *But the test of affection's a Tear.* . . .

Byron's tomb
at Hucknall Torkard

Hucknall Torkard
Church

To be sure, he recognized early on that this kind of thing was not his *forte* (the verse is from *Hours of Idleness*); but in much later lyric work, too, his tone was obviously forced, as it is in his famous poem *The Destruction of Sennacherib*:

> *And the widows of Asshur are loud in their wail,*
> *And the idols are broke in the temple of Baal;*
> *And the might of the Gentile, unsmote by the sword,*
> *Hath melted like snow in the glance of the Lord!*

Shelley was Byron's master in lyric poetry – and even, indeed, in blank verse. Though the latter admired Pope this side idolatry, and Milton only less in spirit, he was impatient to get the sense of his lines down; far too impatient for continual revision, so that his prosody is often limping, and his grammar, even, not impeccable.

Byron's strength is that which Parolles claimed in *All's Well that Ends Well*: 'Simply the thing I am shall make me live'. He was, in everything he wrote, utterly sincere: whether or not he was mistaken, whether or not he was faulty in judgment, whether or not he was unconventional in his notions of private behaviour, he was almost completely sincere – even if in that sincerity he sometimes deceived himself. The virtue sprang from his acute sensitivity: a sensitivity so shattered by his mother's brutal taunts ('lame brat!') that he was afterwards to seek for a substitute in the arms of every woman who came, or would come, his way.

Byron's personality and work

125

With his accession to the title, and his eventual appearance in society – and even more, with the lionization that followed the publication of *Childe Harold* – the handsome and apparently wealthy young man had London and, it seemed, the world at his feet. A career in politics seemed open to him; his career in letters seemed assured; he decided to make a 'good' marriage. But politics proved worthless; his marriage crashed; society turned against him, and he left England. And it is at this point – the point at which he cut himself off from his native country – that he became a really substantial poet.

The first two cantos of *Childe Harold* are entertaining, high-spirited, deftly rhymed and well made. But the second two cantos are infinitely more worth while as poetry. The stanzas on Waterloo and on Napoleon, the verses on the Drachenfels, the description of Clarens, have a deeper tone than anything in the first half of the poem:

> *Roll on, thou deep and dark blue Ocean – Roll!*
> *Ten thousand fleets sweep over thee in vain;*
> *Man marks the earth with ruin – his control*
> *Stops with the shore; upon the watery plain*
> *The wrecks are all thy deed, nor doth remain*
> *A shadow of man's ravage, save his own,*
> *When, for a moment, like a drop of rain,*
> *He sinks into thy depths with bubbling groan,*
> *Without a grave, unknell'd, uncoffin'd and unknown.*

From the moment he left England, too, Byron became the bitterest satirist of his age: he condemned the stupidity of George III and the silly vapid clownings of Prinny; he disdained the mock liberalism of Brougham; he hated Castlereagh – contributing to Hunt's paper a bitter epigram on hearing of his suicide:

> *So He has cut his throat at last! – He! Who?*
> *The man who cut his country's long ago.*

He had no time for Pitt, and wrote his epitaph:

> *With death doom'd to grapple,*
> *Beneath this cold slab, he*
> *Who lied in the Chapel*
> *Now lies in the Abbey.*

He dared to despise Wellington for Waterloo; and one must remember that – even when one was as careless of personal reputation as Byron – it was an act of some courage to publish such sentiments as these, and even more so to publish verses in contradiction of much of the religious feeling of the age. His reputation

The Drachenfels, by Turner   *The castled crag of Drachenfels*
Frowns o'er the wide and winding Rhine,
Whose breast of waters broadly swells
Between the banks which bear the vine. . . .

was consequently such that when, at Mme de Staël's, his name was announced, an English lady novelist fainted dead away.

The force of Byron's political and social opinions, the force of his satire, the romance of his personality, the extraordinary cleverness of his metrical and rhyming schemes, came together finally in *Don Juan*. In that great poem one can find his every virtue (and, I dare say, many of his faults). It was the first, and almost the last, poem of its kind, and in it (as Quiller-Couch puts it) he mounted 'his last grand charge against the forts of hypocrisy and despotism'. *Don Juan* is, like *Childe Harold*, a self-portrait – almost an autobiography; and it is an attractive one.

127

For above all Byron was an attractive figure. His cruelty to his wife arose out of a defect in his very nature; he is scarcely more to be blamed for it than for his 'little foot'. And as to his many affairs: if Lady Caroline and the other women in his life were, or considered themselves, injured – it was always they who had made the first move. Teresa Guiccioli, in her memoirs, left a portrait of the poet which gives some idea of his irresistibility.

Coleridge said that 'if you had seen him you could scarce disbelieve him . . . his eyes the open portals of the sun – things of light and for light.' His behaviour was as frank and candid as those eyes: when he was irritated (as by Hunt and the Yahoos) he showed it; when he was angry, he acted; when he loved, he loved. His compassion was such that even when he was deepest in debt, he set aside each day a sum for charity. He was a man of physical courage, who cared deeply for poetry, and worked at it (as his letters and journals show) with great energy. He had not the spiritual resources of Keats, nor Shelley's singular sweetness of character; but his personality in his poetry is more attractive than either, perhaps because of the light simplicity of his style. As Pascal wrote, 'When we encounter a natural style we are always surprised and delighted, for we thought to see an author and found a man.'

If, finally, he still seems more important as a myth than as a living man, the style of his life is to blame. He lived violently and passionately, yet his life makes sense. He was very like his own description of Rousseau:

> He who threw
> Enchantment over passion, and from woe
> Wrung overwhelming eloquence . . .
> > yet he knew
> How to make madness beautiful, and cast
> O'er erring deeds and thoughts, a heavenly hue.

1788 Byron is born on 22 January at 16 Holles Street, London.

1791 Captain John Byron, the poet's father, dies at Valenciennes, France, on 2 August.

1793 Byron attends his first school, in Broad Street, Aberdeen.

1794–5 Byron attends Aberdeen Grammar School.

1798 On 21 May Byron succeeds to the title of Baron Byron of Rochdale.

1801–5 Byron attends Harrow School.

1803 Byron has his first serious and abortive romance with Mary Chaworth.

1805–7 Byron attends Trinity College, Cambridge.

1806 On 1 November Byron publishes his first collection of verse: *Fugitive Pieces*.

1807 In January *Poems on Various Occasions* and *Hours of Idleness* are published; in March, *Poems Original and Translated*. On 13 March he takes his seat in the House of Lords.

1809 In March *English Bards and Scotch Reviewers* is published, and Byron becomes famous overnight. On 2 July he sails from Falmouth for Lisbon and Seville, Gibraltar, Patras and Athens.

1810 On 3 May Byron makes his famous swim across the Hellespont, and continues his work in Athens, becoming an acute Hellenophile.

1811 On 14 July he returns to England, and in that month his mother dies.

1812 On 27 February he makes the first of only three speeches in the House of Lords: on the Frame Bill. On 10 March the first two cantos of *Childe Harold* are published and Byron becomes immensely fashionable and notorious. He meets Lady Caroline Lamb.

1813 *The Giaour* is published in June, and *The Bride of Abydos* in December.

1814 *The Corsair* comes out in January, and *Lara* in August. On 9 September Byron proposes marriage to Annabella Milbanke.

1815 On 2 January Byron marries Annabella Milbanke at Seaham, County Durham. In April he publishes *Hebrew Melodies*. On 10 December Augusta Ada Byron is born.

1816 On 15 January Byron and Lady Byron part. In February he publishes *The Siege of Corinth* and *Parisina*, and on 21 April signs the separation deed. On 24 April he leaves England for ever, and travels through Brussels and Cologne, arriving on 24 May at Lausanne. On 26 May he meets Shelley. He leaves

Switzerland on 5 October for Milan and Venice. On 18 November the third canto of *Childe Harold* is published, and is followed on 5 December by *The Prisoner of Chillon and other poems*.

1817 On 12 January Byron's daughter is born to Claire Clairmont. Byron, on 29 April, goes for a visit to Rome, and on 14 June moves into the Villa Foscarini, La Mira. On 16 June *Manfred* is published. Newstead Abbey is sold in December for £94,500.

1818 On 22 February *Beppo* is published anonymously. On 9 March Allegra Byron is christened in London, and on 1 May, with the Shelleys and Claire Clairmont, reaches Italy and is sent to Byron. On 28 April *Childe Harold* (Canto IV) is published.

1819 Byron meets Countess Teresa Guiccioli, and on 10 June moves to Ravenna to be near her. On 28 June *Mazeppa* and the *Ode on Venice* are published, followed on 15 July by the first two cantos of *Don Juan* – anonymously.

1821 *The Vision of Judgement* written in October, and in November Byron moves to Pisa. In December the next two cantos of *Don Juan*, *Sardanapalus*, *The Two Foscari* and *Cain* are published.

1822 News of the death of Allegra on 20 April; followed on 7 July by the drowning of Shelley. In September Byron moves to Genoa, where he is joined by Leigh Hunt, in the first issue of whose journal *The Liberal* Byron's *Vision of Judgement* is published on 15 October. *Werner* is published on 22 November.

1823 On 15 July Byron sails for Greece, and on 2 August anchors off Cephalonia. In December he sails for Missolonghi.

1824 On 4 January Byron joins Prince Mavrocordatos at Missolonghi, where he begins training a small army of mercenaries. On 9 April he catches a chill while out riding, and on 19 April dies. Brought back to England, he is buried on 16 July at Hucknall Torkard, near Nottingham.

NOTES ON THE PICTURES

*The details in square brackets refer to the derivation of caption quotations,
which are from Byron unless otherwise stated.*

Frontispiece: PORTRAIT OF BYRON by Vincenzo Camuccini (1773–1844), probably painted in Rome in 1815. *Galleria di S. Luca, Rome. Photo Mansell-Anderson.*

5 NEWSTEAD ABBEY, *c.* 1720. From *The Works of Lord Byron*, 1898–1901, ed. R.E. Prothero. [*Childe Harold*, I, vii.]

6 BATH, The Circus, 1784. *British Museum.*

7 MRS BYRON. Painted perhaps between 1803 and 1811, by J. Ramsay. From *The Works of Lord Byron*, op. cit. [Letter to Henrietta d'Ussières, 8 June 1814.]

8 BYRON'S BIRTHPLACE, 16 Holles Street, off Cavendish Square; the street was demolished during the 1939–45 war. *Illustrated London News*, 28 January 1888.

ST MARYLEBONE CHURCH, 1750. Engraving by J. Roberts after Chatelain. *British Museum.*

9 CASTLE STREET, ABERDEEN, 1812. Engraving by C. Turner after H. Irvine. *British Museum.*

10 BYRON AGED SEVEN. A miniature painted in 1795. *By permission of Harrow School.* [*I Would I Were a Careless Child*, iii.]

11 ABERDEEN GRAMMAR SCHOOL as it was between 1757 and 1863. *Bon Record: Records and Reminiscences of Aberdeen Grammar School*, 1906. ['*My Dictionary*', May 1821. Byron goes on: 'I had a very serious,

saturnine, but kind young man, named Paterson, for a Tutor. . . . With him I began Latin in Ruddiman's Grammar, and continued till I went to the "Grammar School" (*Scotice* "Schule" – *Aberdonice* "Squeel"), where I threaded all the Classes to the Fourth, when I was recalled to England (where I had been hatched) by the demise of my Uncle.']

12–13 NEWSTEAD ABBEY, 1834. Etched by L. Haghe after M. Webster. *Newstead Abbey Collections. Reproduced by kind permission of the City Librarian of Nottingham.* Newstead perhaps never looked as tidy as this during Byron's residence; but that, especially as an adolescent, he was deeply impressed by its romantic air and history is obvious from the two indifferent but enthusiastic poems he wrote about the Abbey. [*Elegy on Newstead Abbey*, i.]

14 DULWICH, 1860. At the time when this watercolour by J.C. Mandy was painted, Dulwich was still – as in Byron's time – a village some seven miles from the city. *Guildhall Library. Photo John Webb, Brompton Studio.*

HARROW CHURCH AND SCHOOL from the cricket grounds, 1816. R. Ackermann's *History of the Colleges*, 1816. *Guildhall Library. Photo John Webb, Brompton Studio.* [*On a Distant View of the Village and School of Harrow on the Hill*, iii.]

15 HARROW SCHOOL-ROOM. R. Ackermann, op. cit. *Guildhall Library. Photo John Webb,*

131

Brompton Studio. [Letter to his mother, *c.* 1804. Boys were commonly up at 5.30 a.m. and in chapel by 6; they then worked at Greek or Latin for three hours before a breakfast of 'bread, stinking butter, and beer or milk'. Then another two hours composing Latin verses before an hour of games, and lunch of mutton, or bread and cheese. More work until dinner: a cut off the joint, bread and beer. Another hour of work, and bed at 9 p.m. As for the masters, in Southey's opinion, 'All that have ever fallen under my knowledge are illiterate, savage and unrelenting. They endeavour, by discipline to sour the temper and break the spirit of their unfortunate subjects, who in their turn exercise the same tyranny over their inferiors, till the hall of learning becomes only a seminary for brutality.']

16 HARROW CHURCHYARD. Engraved by Edward Finden after C. Stanfield. The brothers Edward and William Finden devoted many years to preparing a series of engravings of portraits and scenes of people and places associated with Byron: the collection, *Illustrations of the Life and Works of Lord Byron*, was published in 1833. [Letter to John Murray, 26 May 1822.]

17 MARY CHAWORTH. Anonymous miniature. *Newstead Abbey Collections. Reproduced by kind permission of the City Librarian of Nottingham.* [*The Dream*, II, 1.58.]

AUGUSTA LEIGH. By G. Hayter. *By courtesy the Trustees of the British Museum.* [*Stanzas to Augusta*, IV.]

18 GREAT COURT AND CHAPEL of Trinity College, Cambridge. By Thomas Malton, 1798. *British Museum.*

19 LORD BYRON AT CAMBRIDGE, engraved by F. W. Hunt after Gilchrist, 1871. *Newstead Abbey Collections. Reproduced by*

kind permission of the City Librarian of Nottingham.

20 'BON TON'. A contemporary cartoon. The woman is probably intended for Lady Caroline Lamb; Love was a fashionable jeweller of the period. *By courtesy the Trustees of the British Museum.*

21 A FOUNTAIN in the cloisters at Newstead. Edward Finden after W. Westall. *Newstead Abbey Collections. Reproduced by kind permission of the City Librarian of Nottingham.* [Nanny Smith in conversation with Washington Irving, *Letters*, Vol. III, *Journal of Rutgers University Library*, 1946.]

22 VIEW OF THE HOUSE OF LORDS and Commons from Old Palace Yard, 1821. Painted and engraved by R. Havell. *British Museum.*

23 'THE GLENARVON GHOST at the Masquerade'. An illustration to Harriette Wilson's *Memoirs*, related to Lady Caroline Lamb's novel *Glenarvon*, in which she painted a colourful 'portrait' of Byron. Harriette Wilson describes a meeting with Byron at a masquerade: 'He was habited in a dark brown flowing robe, which was confined round the waist by a leathern belt, and fell in ample folds to the ground. . . . His attitude was graceful in the extreme. His whole countenance so bright, severe, and beautiful, that I should have been afraid to have loved him.' *By courtesy the Trustees of the British Museum.*

24 BYRON AND ROBERT RUSHTON, engraved after a painting by George Sanders. *Newstead Abbey Collections. Reproduced by kind permission of the City Librarian of Nottingham.* [*Childe Harold*, III, xiii.] The painting was probably painted in May 1808, and may have cost Byron as much as 250 guineas, since Sanders was an extremely fashionable painter.

25 FALMOUTH HARBOUR, engraved by T.G. Lipton after J.M.W. Turner. *Victoria and Albert Museum, London.* [*Lines to Mr Hodgson, written on board the Lisbon Packet,* v.]

LISBON FROM FORT ALMEIDA, engraved by Edward Finden after C. Stanfield. *Finden's Illustrations,* op. cit. [*Childe Harold,* I, xvi.]

26 MRS BYRON. By T. Stewardson. *In the possession of John Murray.* [Letter to Augusta, 23 April 1805.]

27 PLAZA SAN FRANCISCO, Seville, 1838. Engraved by L. Haghe after G. Vivian. *Victoria and Albert Museum, London.* [*Childe Harold,* I, xlvi; but this is at least in part melodrama, for in a letter to his mother (11 August 1809) Byron writes: 'Seville is a beautiful town; though the streets are narrow, they are clean.']

28 TEMPLE OF JUPITER OLYMPUS, Athens. Engraved by William Finden after C. Stanfield. *Finden's Illustrations,* op. cit. [*Childe Harold,* II, x.]

ALI PASHA, late Vizier of Jannina. Engraved by William Finden after F. Stone. *Finden's Illustrations,* op. cit. [Letter to Mrs Byron, 12 November 1809.] To be a son of the Vizier had, however, its drawbacks. When his son Mouctar was suspected of infidelity, Ali Pasha had fifteen of the most beautiful women of Jannina seized, tied up in sacks, and thrown into the lake, in the pious belief that one of them might be Mouctar's mistress.

29 BYRON in Albanian costume. *National Portrait Gallery, London.* Byron was sitting for this portrait between March and May, 1814, to Thomas Phillips. On 3 May 1814, he sent the costume to Miss Mercer Elphinstone, an acquaintance, to wear at a masquerade. 'It is put off and on in a few minutes', he wrote; 'If you like the dress, keep it.' This costume is now in the Museum of Costume, at the Assembly Rooms, Bath. [Letter to Mrs Byron, 12 November 1809.]

30 THE MAID OF ATHENS. An illustration from *The Byron Gallery,* 1833, by C.R. Cockerell. When the artists of the early nineteenth century were not drawing vicious and scurrilous cartoons of Byron (cf. pp. 53, 54, 57), they were drawing ludicrously sentimental illustrations to his life and work, of which this (and that on p. 71) is an example. [*Maid of Athens,* iv.]

31 SMYRNA from the Jews' Burial Ground. Watercolour by W.J. Müller, c. 1840. *By courtesy the Trustees of the British Museum.*

THE CAPUCHIN CONVENT, Athens. Engraved by Edward Finden, after C. Stanfield. *Finden's Illustrations,* op. cit.

32 BOATSWAIN, Byron's Newfoundland dog. Painting by Clifton Thomson, 1803. *Newstead Abbey Collections. Reproduced by kind permission of the City Librarian of Nottingham.* Byron built him a tomb, which he placed as nearly as possible on the site of the altar of Newstead Abbey. [Inscription on Boatswain's tomb at Newstead, 11. 25–26.]

33 'CHILDE HAROLD'S PILGRIMAGE' by J.M.W. Turner; Italy, c. 1832. *Courtesy the Trustees of the Tate Gallery.* [*Childe Harold,* IV, xxxii.]

34 NOTTINGHAM. Engraved by T.A. Prior after K. Johnson. *Mansell Collection.* [Letter to Lord Holland, 25 February 1812. Writing about the Frame Bill, coming up for debate in the House of Lords, Byron continued: 'The maintenance and

well-doing of the industrious poor is an object of greater consequence to the community than the enrichment of a few monopolists by any improvement in the implements of trade, which deprives the workman of his bread, and renders the labourer "unworthy of his hire".']

HOLLAND HOUSE, south side. Engraved by P. H. Delamotte. *Photo National Buildings Record.* Badly damaged during the 1939–45 war, Holland House, by a criminal act of neglect, was allowed to become irreparable. The south façade is still intact, and one wing, extensively rebuilt, is in use as a Youth Hostel. Open-air performances of opera and ballet are, in the summer, presented on a stage in front of this façade.

35 HENRY FOX, 3rd Baron Holland, 1795, by F. Fabre. *National Portrait Gallery.*

WILLIAM LAMB, later Lord Melbourne, by T. Lawrence. *In the possession of the late Lady Hambleden's children.* Lamb (1779–1848), twice Prime Minister and at the end of his life an adviser to Queen Victoria, was charming, cultured and affable; yet was responsible for the transportation of the six Tolpuddle labourers for attempts to establish trade unionism.

36 LADY CAROLINE LAMB in page's costume. An anonymous miniature. *In the possession of John Murray.* [Letter to Lady Caroline, *c.* 1812.]

37 LADY CAROLINE LAMB on horseback. An anonymous watercolour. *By permission of Mary Duchess of Roxburghe.* [Letter to Lady Melbourne, 26 June 1814.]

38 JANE ELIZABETH, COUNTESS OF OXFORD, 1797, by J. Hoppner. *Courtesy the Trustees of the Tate Gallery.*

LADY MELBOURNE. A mezzotint after Sir Joshua Reynolds. *Photo Courtauld Institute of Art.* In his Journal for 24 November 1813, Byron wrote: 'If she had been a few years younger, what a fool she would have made of me, had she thought it worth her while, – and I should have lost a valuable and most agreeable *friend*. Mem. – a mistress never is nor can be a friend. While you agree, you are lovers; and, when it is over, anything but friends.'

MELBOURNE HOUSE, Whitehall, by T. Malton. *By courtesy the Trustees of the British Museum.* Lady Caroline Lamb gave waltzing parties there, but discontinued them when she discovered that Byron could not dance. Before William Lamb's occupation of it, the house (now the Scottish Office) was the residence of the Duke of York.

39 BYRON aged twenty-five. Engraved by R. Grave after James Holmes. Said to be the last portrait made of him in England, in 1813. *Newstead Abbey Collections. Reproduced by kind permission of the City Librarian of Nottingham.*

40 'THE BRIDE OF ABYDOS', an illustration to the poem, by H. J. Richter: *Come, lay thy head upon my breast/And I will kiss thee into rest* [I, xi]. *Newstead Abbey Collections. Reproduced by kind permission of the City Librarian of Nottingham.*

41 'HIGH LIFE AT ALMACK'S': A cartoon by P. Egan (*Life in London*, 1821).

42 ANNABELLA MILBANKE aged twenty. By G. Hayter, 1812. From *The Works of Lord Byron*, op. cit. [*Literary Life*, 1865, by the Rev. Mr Harness.]

43 NEWSTEAD, *c.* 1828. Anon. engraving. *Photo National Buildings Record.*

44 JUDITH MILBANKE, 1784, by J. Downman. *By kind permission of the Earl of Lytton.*

RALPH MILBANKE, 1778, by Sir Joshua Reynolds. *By kind permission of the Earl of Lytton.*

SEAHAM HARBOUR, from *View of the County Palatine of Durham*, 1834, by E. Mackenzie and M. Ross. [Letter to Thomas Moore, 2 February 1815.]

45 BYRON aged twenty-six. By Thomas Phillips, 1814. *Newstead Abbey Collections. Reproduced by kind permission of the City Librarian of Nottingham.* [The Rev. Mr Harness, op. cit.; Preface to *Julian and Maddalo*, 1824.]

46 HALNABY HALL, by F. Peake. The Hall was demolished in 1953, and the grounds and surrounding woodlands despoiled. Some renovation has taken place; the surviving wing of the Hall contains offices. [Letter to Lady Melbourne, 3 January 1815.]

47 THOMAS MOORE, from *Fraser's Magazine*, October 1830. Moore (1779–1852) became a sort of Irish laureate, and became famous for *Lalla Rookh* (1817), a collection of versified anecdotes connected by a prose narrative. He joined Byron in satirizing the Regent. [*To Thomas Moore*, i.]

48 AUGUSTA LEIGH, by T.C. Wageman. *Newstead Abbey Collections. Reproduced by kind permission of the City Librarian of Nottingham.*

49 NEWMARKET, 1842. *British Museum.* Six Mile Bottom lies about six miles south-west of Newmarket.

50 PICCADILLY from Hyde Park Turnpike, with Piccadilly Terrace on the left, by Ackermann. *Guildhall Library. Photo John Webb, Brompton Studio.*

51 GEORGE ('BEAU') BRUMMELL, engraved from a miniature, by John Cook. *By courtesy the Trustees of the British Museum.* [Max Beerbohm, *Dandies and Dandies*, 1896.]

THE DANDY CLUB, 1818. A cartoon by Richard Dighton. *By courtesy the Trustees of the British Museum.* [Letter to the Earl of Blessington, 14 April 1823. In his *Detached Thoughts*, 1821, Byron remarks: 'I liked the Dandies; they were always very civil to *me*, though in general they disliked literary people. . . . The truth is, though I gave up the business early, I had a tinge of Dandyism in my minority, and probably retained enough of it to conciliate the great ones. . . . I had gamed, and drank, and taken my degrees in most dissipations.']

52 NOTICE OF THE SALE of Newstead Abbey by auction, 28 July 1815. *Newstead Abbey Collections. Reproduced by kind permission of the City Librarian of Nottingham.* [*Recollections of a Long Life*, 1909–11, by John Cam Hobhouse (Lord Broughton).]

53 'LOBBY LOUNGERS', taken from the saloon of Drury Lane Theatre. By I.R. Cruikshank, 1816. *By courtesy the Trustees of the British Museum.* Among the women ogled by Byron (left), and other men, is (holding a muff) Mrs Mardyn, who also appears in the cartoons on pp. 54 and 57. Public rumour suggested a romance between this handsome young actress and Byron; while there is no evidence to support this, neither is there any evidence to disprove it.

'A BUZ IN A BOX, or the Poet in a Pet': the opening of the New Drury Lane Theatre, 1812. Byron had composed a set of verses for the opening; these were, to say the least, inadequate, and the press recognized the fact. *By courtesy the Trustees of the British Museum.*

54 'FASHIONABLES of 1816 taking the air in Hyde Park!' by I.R. Cruikshank. *By courtesy the Trustees of the British Museum.*

55 KIRKBY MALLORY HALL, from *History and Antiquities of the County of Leicester,* Vol. IV, Pt. 2 (1811), by J. Nichols. [Letter to Augusta Leigh, October 1820.]

56 WILLIAM GODWIN, by James Northcote, 1802. *National Portrait Gallery, London.* [From the anon. caption to a Gillray cartoon, *The Anti-Jacobin Magazine,* 1798.]

CLAIRE CLAIRMONT, by A. Curran, 1819. *Newstead Abbey Collections. Reproduced by kind permission of the City Librarian of Nottingham.*

57 'THE SEPARATION' by I.R. Cruikshank. 'Sketch from the Private Life of Lord Iron who panegyrized his wife but satirized her confidante.' Byron has his arms around Mrs Mardyn (cf. note 53 above). Lady Byron holds the infant Ada, and on her arm is James Perry, Editor of *The Morning Chronicle,* who was not one of Byron's admirers. The scowling old woman is Mrs Clermont, who had been Lady Byron's governess, had been promoted to the position of confidante, and whom Byron largely blamed for the separation, pouring scorn on her in *A Sketch. By courtesy the Trustees of the British Museum.*

'FARE THEE WELL' by I.R. Cruikshank. Byron clasps the waist of Mrs Mardyn, and waves to Lady Byron, dimly seen, Ada in her arms, on the shore. The other women are Drury Lane actresses. *By courtesy the Trustees of the British Museum.* [Thomas Medwin, in *Journal of the Conversations of Lord Byron,* 1824, quotes him thus; and although it is clear that Byron overemphasized the degree of public feeling against him, it is also true (cf. these and other cartoons) that some sections of the right-wing Press attacked him virulently.]

58 AUGUSTA LEIGH, 1817, by James Holmes. *By kind permission of the Earl of Lytton.*

59 DOVER HARBOUR, 1827, by J. Carpenter. *Victoria and Albert Museum, London.* [John Cam Hobhouse in his Diary, quoted in *Byron,* 1957, by Leslie A. Marchand.]

HÔTEL DE VILLE, Brussels, by Samuel Prout. *Victoria and Albert Museum, London.*

60 THE DUKE OF WELLINGTON's headquarters at Waterloo. Engraved by C. Turner after Capt. Jones. *By courtesy the Trustees of the British Museum.*

61 BYRON aged twenty-eight. By G.H. Harlow, 1816. *Henry E. Huntington Library and Art Gallery, San Marino, California.* The dating of this sketch is unclear: the artist seems to have dated it 1816; but Byron himself referred to it as having been drawn in 1818, on 6 August – on the same day that Harlow drew Margarita Cogni (see p. 74).

COLOGNE, by Samuel Prout. *Victoria and Albert Museum, London.*

62 A VIEW OF CLARENS on Lake Geneva, engraved by Née after Brandoin. *Photo Hachette.*

THE VILLA DIODATI, engraved by Edward Finden after W. Purser. *Finden's Illustrations,* op. cit.

63 DR J.W. POLIDORI, by F.G. Gainsford. *National Portrait Gallery, London.* [Letter to Thomas Moore, 6 November 1816.]

64 CHÂTEAU DE CHILLON, 1826. Lithograph by Engelmann after Villeneuve. *Victoria and Albert Museum, London.* [*The Prisoner of Chillon,* VI.]

65 P.B. SHELLEY, by A. Curran, 1819. *National Portrait Gallery, London.* [Letter to Thomas Moore, 4 March 1822.]

66 MADAME DE STAËL, by F. Gerard. *Musée de Versailles. Photo Giraudon.* A French novelist and essayist, she (1766–1817) was deeply interested in politics, fought a fascinating verbal duel with Napoleon, and published several noteworthy books of which *Corinne*, 1807, 'an aesthetic romance', is perhaps the best. [Journal, 16 November 1813.]

67 CHÂTEAU DE COPPET, by Brun. *Bibliothèque publique et universitaire, Geneva.* Coppet was Madame de Staël's home for some years.

68 'GENT – NO GENT – REGENT!!' by George Cruikshank. *By courtesy the Trustees of the British Museum.* The first section shows the Prince Regent as the handsome officer which Lawrence's splendid portrait at the Brighton Pavilion depicts; the second shows him in 'The Cock and Hen Club' with Mrs Fitzherbert, his wife, and low company; the third, a gouty wreck in the Pavilion at Brighton, surrounded by Chinoiserie and sycophants. The cartoon was published in 1816.

69 LA SCALA, MILAN, 1818–20, by Angeli. *Museo Teatrale alla Scala, Milan.* [Letter to Thomas Moore, 6 November 1816. It was at the Scala that Byron re-encountered Polidori, who was arrested there for brawling with an Austrian officer. Byron stood bail; but Polidori was banished from Milan.]

70 BYRON AND MARIANNA SEGATI, anon. *Newstead Abbey Collections. Reproduced by kind permission of the City Librarian of Nottingham.* Another fictitious romantic illustration (cf. note 30). [Letter to Thomas Moore, 24 December 1816.]

71 THE ARMENIAN MONASTERY, San Lazzaro, by C. Reichardt. *Biblioteca Armena, S. Lazzaro.* Presumably an imaginary portrait of Byron, but in an authentic setting.

THE COLLEONI STATUE, Venice, by James Holland. *The Lord and Lady Walston, Newton Park, Cambridge.*

72 CARNIVAL IN VENICE. The Piazza S. Marco. Anon. *Museo Correr, Venice.*

73 AN EXECUTION for murder in Rome, 1820. From R. Bridgens: *Sketches Illustrative of the Manners and Customs of France, Switzerland and Italy,* 1821, with a text by Polidori.

THE BRIDGE OF SIGHS, Venice, by Samuel Prout. *Victoria and Albert Museum, London.*

74 MARGARITA COGNI, engraved by H.T. Ryall after G.H. Harlow. *Finden's Illustrations,* op. cit. [Letter to Augusta Leigh, 21 September 1818. It is worth noting that this mild little portrait is contradicted by every report of Byron's, who called her 'wild as a witch and fierce as a demon'; when he finally dismissed her, she threw herself into a canal – but was rescued before coming to any great harm.]

75 THE VILLA FOSCARINI, La Mira, by J.F. Costa. *Photo Vasari, Rome.* The Villa was originally a convent, and in the seventeenth century became the home of the Foscarini family.

ALLEGRA, painted by an anonymous artist in Venice in 1818, when she was eighteen months old. *In the possession of John Murray.* [Letter to Augusta, July 1818, in the University of Texas; quoted by Marchand in *Byron,* op. cit.]

76 BYRON in the Palazzo Mocenigo, painted

in 1839 by J. Scarlett Davis. *Henry E. Huntington Library and Art Gallery, San Marino, California.* The figure of Byron is, of course, idealized.

77 THE VENETIAN LAGOON, by Guardi. *Reproduced by permission of the Syndics of the Fitzwilliam Museum, Cambridge.*

THE RIALTO, 1818, by J. M. W. Turner. *Private collection.*

78 'A NOBLE POET scratching up His Ideas.' A cartoon, published in 1823. Behind Byron's head, a picture entitled *End of Abel* refers to *Cain*, published in 1821. *By courtesy the Trustees of the British Museum.*

79 BYRON, 1818. Engraved by E. Scriven after G. H. Harlow (cf. note 60). *Newstead Abbey Collections. Reproduced by kind permission of the City Librarian of Nottingham.*

80 TERESA GUICCIOLI aged eighteen, engraved after E. C. Wood. From *The Byron Gallery*, 1833, op. cit. [Letter to Augusta Leigh, 26 July 1819.]

81 PALAZZO GUICCIOLI, Ravenna, by A. Alessandri. From *The Works of Lord Byron*, op. cit.

SET FOR 'OTELLO' at La Scala, Milan, designed by Alessandro Sanguirico, who also designed for the Fenice in Venice, where Byron saw Rossini's opera – a brilliant piece revived successfully in Rome in 1964. *Museo Teatrale alla Scala, Milan.*

83 BOLOGNA, 1826, by Richard Bonington (1802–28) – that most unjustly neglected of English painters so admired by Delacroix. *Collection of Mr and Mrs Paul Mellon.*

84 DANTE'S TOMB at Ravenna, by S. Prout. *Finden's Illustrations*, op. cit.

85 COUNT PIETRO GAMBA. Drawn by Count d'Orsay. *From the Cini Gamba collection at Filetto, destroyed by fire during the 1939–45 war.* [Letter to Teresa Guiccioli, quoted by Iris Origo.]

86 A MEETING OF THE CARBONARI, from B. Bertoldi's *Memoirs of the Secret Societies*, 1821. [Diary, 18 February 1821.]

87 THE VILLA GAMBA, Filetto. *By kind permission of Marchesa Origo.*

NAPLES, 1820. Constitutional troops, led by Pepe and Minichini, enter the city. Painting by M. Riscendes. *Museo di S. Martino, Naples.*

88 'THE DEATH OF SARDANAPALUS', by Eugène Delacroix, 1827. *Louvre, Paris. Photo Bulloz.* Delacroix (1798–1863) greatly admired Byron, whose poetry inspired him to paint several wonderful canvases of Venice, which he himself never visited. His painting of the death of Sardanapalus reveals an imperfect knowledge of Byron's drama; for the King of Nineveh in fact dies on a funeral pyre, and not (as this canvas suggests) calmly surveying acts of varied carnage in his harem.

90 'CAIN AND ABEL.' From *A Family Bible*, 1735. Engraved by J. Smith.

91 PISA from the Campo Santo, by J. Arnout. *Victoria and Albert Museum, London.*

92 ROBERT SOUTHEY, by H. Edridge. *National Portrait Gallery, London.* [Preface to *The Vision of Judgement*.]

93 VILLA LANFRANCHI, Pisa, by O. F. M. Ward. From *The Works of Lord Byron*, op. cit.

94 EDWARD AND JANE WILLIAMS. Both portraits by G. Clint. *The Curators of the Bodleian Library.*

95 BYRON at Pisa, 1822, engraved by C. Turner after W. E. West. *Newstead Abbey Collections. Reproduced by kind permission of the City Librarian of Nottingham.* Byron, in a letter to Moore (27 August 1822), remarks that he 'sat for my picture to young West, an American artist . . . for the New York Academy, I believe.' [Shelley in a letter to Horatio Smith, 14 September 1821.]

96 EDWARD JOHN TRELAWNY, by Joseph Severn, 1838. *National Portrait Gallery, London.* [Byron's *mot* is reported by R. Glynn Grylls in her *Trelawny*; if it lacks authenticity, it is probably as accurate as most of Trelawny's anecdotes.]

97 THE CASA MAGNI, San Terenzo: Shelley's house across the bay from Lerici. *Keats–Shelley Memorial House, Rome.*

99 THE 'DON JUAN' AND THE 'BOLIVAR', sketched by E. E. Williams. *By courtesy the Trustees of the British Museum.* [Quoted by Trelawny in his *Recollections*, op. cit.]

100 MARY SHELLEY, by R. Rothwell, 1841. *National Portrait Gallery, London.* [Mary Shelley's *Journal* for Shelley's birthday, 4 August 1821.]

101 LERICI – THE CASTLE, by Richard Bonington. *Collection of Mrs William Bernard. At present on loan to the Castle Museum, Nottingham.*

102 THE ALBARO HILL, Genoa, where the Casa Saluzzo stood. Engraved by Guidotti. *British Museum.*

103 LEIGH HUNT, from *Fraser's Magazine*, June 1834. Hunt (1784–1859) was per-haps the greatest critical supporter of Shelley and Keats, and a notable essayist and critic. [Letter to Thomas Moore, 1 June 1818.]

COUNT D'ORSAY. 'A very handsome companion, in the shape of a "French Count" (to use Farquhar's phrase in *The Beaux Stratagem*) who has all the air of a *Cupidon déchaîné*, and is one of the few specimens I have seen of our ideal of a Frenchman *before* the Revolution.' – Byron in a letter to Moore, 2 April 1823. Engraved by F. C. Lewis after F. Grant. *By courtesy the Trustees of the British Museum.*

104 THE TEMPORARY ELGIN ROOM at the British Museum, 1819. By A. Archer. *British Museum.* [Keats' sonnet *On Seeing the Elgin Marbles*.]

105 LADY BLESSINGTON. Engraved by H. T. Ryall after A. E. Chalon. *Newstead Abbey Collections. Reproduced by kind permission of the City Librarian of Nottingham.*

BYRON AT GENOA, sketched by Count d'Orsay, 1823. *Newstead Abbey Collections. Reproduced by kind permission of the City Librarian of Nottingham.*

107 APOTHEOSIS OF SIMON BOLIVAR, by T. Salas. *Acervo Historico, Caracas.*

LOUIS XVIII leaving the Tuileries on the night of 19–20 March 1815, by A. J. Gros. *Musée de Versailles. Photo Giraudon.*

108 LORD BLESSINGTON, by J. Holmes. *National Portrait Gallery, London.*

LORD DOUGLAS KINNAIRD, anon. *In the possession of the Master of Kinnaird.*

109 BYRON, by Bouvier, wearing the helmet he had designed. *Newstead Abbey Collections. Reproduced by kind permission of the City*

Librarian of Nottingham. [*Childe Harolde*, III, xxii.]

110 ARGOSTOLI, Cephalonia, by H. Cook. *British Museum.*

111 BYRON and Lyon, the Newfoundland given Byron by a retired Naval lieutenant. From *The Last Days of Lord Byron*, 1825, by W. Parry. [Byron reported by Parry, ibid.]

112 TERESA GUICCIOLI, by Bartolini. *By kind permission of Marchesa Origo.* [Letter to Teresa Guiccioli, 29 October 1823. Byron's last communication to her.]

113 VATHI, Ithaca, by C. Bentley, 1839. *Victoria and Albert Museum.*

LORD BYRON attended by his Suliote Guards, from W. Parry, op. cit.

114 BYRON'S HOUSE at Missolonghi, from W. Parry, op. cit. This engraving is described as 'much idealized'. The house was in fact of three floors; Byron lived on the second floor, which had a bedroom and sitting-room besides three additional rooms for the servants.

116 AUGUSTA ADA BYRON, from *The Works of Lord Byron*, op. cit.

117 ODYSSEUS TRITZO (also known as Ulysses), from *Harper's Magazine*, 1893–4. One of the leaders of the military faction that forced the resignation of Mavrocordatos from the Presidency late in 1823.

PRINCE ALEXANDER MAVROCORDATOS, from *Harper's Magazine*, 1893–4. Elected first President of Greece, 1822. But the government was weak and easily split; Mavrocordatos was a leader of the civil group, which included the Primates and civil dignitaries.

119 'GREECE expiring on the Ruins of Missolonghi', 1827, by Eugène Delacroix. *Musée des Beaux-Arts, Bordeaux. Photo Giraudon.* [*Don Juan*, III.]

121 TITLE-PAGE of Byron's funeral oration, delivered in Greek by Spiridion Tricoupi, son of a Primate of Missolonghi, at the funeral there on 19 April 1824. Later published in Paris. *British Museum.*

JOHN MURRAY. Anon. *Newstead Abbey Collections. Reproduced by kind permission of the City Librarian of Nottingham.*

122 JOHN CAM HOBHOUSE, later Baron Broughton. Engraved by C. Turner after J. Lonsdale. *By courtesy the Trustees of the British Museum.* Hobhouse (1786–1869) was Byron's literary executor.

123 BROCKET HALL, the home of Lady Caroline Lamb. By P. Sandby. *Victoria and Albert Museum, London.*

124 BYRON'S TOMB at Hucknall Torkard. Augusta Leigh later added a marble relief portrait. The entrance to the tomb is on the right-hand side of the chancel, at approximately the point where the figure on the right of the engraving stands. *Newstead Abbey Collections. Reproduced by kind permission of the City Librarian of Nottingham.*

125 HUCKNALL TORKARD CHURCH, near Nottingham. The town is now generally known simply as 'Hucknall'. From *The Letters and Journals of Lord Byron*, edited by T. Moore, 1833.

127 THE DRACHENFELS, by Turner. *Courtauld Institute Galleries, Spooner Bequest.* [*Childe Harold*, III.]

Tailpiece: BYRON'S CREST – from his helmet.

BIBLIOGRAPHICAL NOTE

More perhaps than any other English poet, Byron reveals himself through his own writing, so that the texts of his poems, letters and journals are of paramount importance. The great 1899 edition of the *Poetical Works* edited by Ernest Hartley Coleridge is still, fortunately, in print – and in one volume. Peter Quennell in 1950 made a comprehensive collection of Byron's letters and journals – although it is to be hoped that previously censored material will eventually be made fully accessible. Mr Quennell's edition, in two volumes, is entitled *Byron: A Self-portrait*. A selection of the letters is also available in the Everyman series, as are some of the poems.

Of the various biographies, by far the most complete is that by Leslie A. Marchant (three volumes, 1957). There are other works published in this century which are of interest; only a few of them can be suggested here –

GRYLLS, R. Glynn: *Claire Clairmont* (1939); *Trelawny* (1950)
JENKINS, Elizabeth: *Lady Caroline Lamb* (1932)
KNIGHT, G. Wilson: *Lord Byron's Marriage* (1957)
MAUROIS, André: *Byron* (1930)
ORIGO, Iris: *The Last Attachment* (1949)
VINCENT, E.R.: *Byron, Hobhouse and Foscolo* (1949)
WHITE, Newman Ivey: *Shelley* (2 vols., 1947)

The memoirs of Byron's contemporaries and friends provide an endless pattern of memories, some more reliable than others. The most important of these memoirs (some of which, unfortunately, are out of print) are:

DALLAS, R.C.: *Correspondence of Lord Byron with a Friend* (1825)
GAMBA, Count Pietro: *A Narrative of Lord Byron's Last Journey to Greece* (1825)
GUICCIOLI, Countess Teresa: *My Recollections of Lord Byron* (1869)
HUNT, LEIGH: *Lord Byron and Some of His Contemporaries* (1828)
KENNEDY, James: *Conversations on Religion with Lord Byron* (1830)
LAMB, Lady Caroline: *Glenarvon* (3 vols., 1816)
MILLINGEN, James: *Memoirs of the Affairs of Greece* (1831)
MOORE, Thomas: *The Life, Letters and Journal of Lord Byron* (1892)
POLIDORI, John William: *The Diary of John William Polidori* (ed. W.M. Rossetti, 1911)
SHELLEY, Mary: *The Letters of Mary W. Shelley* (1944); *Mary Shelley's Journal* (1947)
STOWE, Harriet Beecher: *Lady Byron Vindicated* (1870)
TRELAWNY, Edward John: *Records of Shelley, Byron and the Author* (1887); *Recollections of the Last Days of Shelley and Byron* (1858)

INDEX

Numbers in italics refer to the illustrations